From our emotional wounds of the past come our distorted images of God. These, in turn, cause emotional and spiritual damage. In these pages, William and Kristi Gaultiere explore fourteen "mistaken identities" that people attribute to God. You will see how they relate to common emotional problems, such as depression, low self-esteem, or perfectionism. With a revealing "God Image Questionnaire," counsel, and probing questions, *Mistaken Identity* will guide you into the realization you are His beloved child.

"From the moment Bill and Kristi walked into our Christian Leaders and Speakers Seminars I knew they were an exceptional couple ... on an exceptional mission: they wanted to show the world who God is and how He can be real in each life. They have done it brilliantly and personally and have given a creative, insightful look at how to overcome the troubled perceptions of God that cause emotional and spiritual distress for so many Christians today."

Florence Littauer, author, President and Founder, Class Speakers

"Mistaken Identity *places the focus on God's image, where it needs to be if one is really concerned about understanding their own self-image and self-esteem.... An excellent treatment on how to integrate what we know about God's parenting and human parenting."*

Richard J. Mohline, Dean of Administration
Rosemead School of Psychology

"So many of our problems in life are complicated by the hurts we experience in our perception of God, and we limit Him when we need Him the most. The Gaultieres address this issue and provide a helpful tool for anyone involved in a counseling ministry."

David Stoop, author of *Self-Talk: Key to Personal Growth*

Mistaken Identity

William and Kristi Gaultiere

Power Books
Fleming H. Revell Company
Old Tappan, New Jersey

Library of Congress Cataloging-in-Publication Data

Gaultiere, William.
Mistaken identity / William and Kristi Gaultiere.
p. cm.
ISBN 0-8007-5295-3
1. God—Love. I. Gaultiere, Kristi. II. Title.
BT140.G38 1989
231′.6—dc19 88-30188
CIP

Published by the Fleming H. Revell Company
Old Tappan, New Jersey 07675
Printed in the United States of America

To our mentors,
especially Cara and Bill,
who invested in each of our
lives and in our marriage.

Contents

Foreword

If you are interested in knowing God's love—I mean *really* knowing His love for you—then you must read *Mistaken Identity*. It will open the very depths of your soul to the possibility of being loved by God. And for this my heart leaps to its feet and applauds! It is written by Bill and Kristi Gaultiere who have worked for me at the Crystal Cathedral as college pastors and as Christian counselors. I have found that they minister to people with a rare combination of sensitive spiritual concern and profound psychological insight.

The positive message of hope in this book is one that people need to hear today. I know because I have talked to literally thousands of people across the world, holding their hands and looking into their eyes, and I've found that what they really want is to be loved. Yet, time and again my heart is saddened when I hear that these people feel distanced from God's love. They want so badly to experience God's love and to know that they are beautiful people in His eyes, but their painful life experiences lead them to doubt His love for them. Bill and Kristi Gaultiere have risen to the challenge by showing you how to discover God's love even when you are troubled by life's greatest difficulties.

Mistaken Identity hits the nail right on the head! Bill and Kristi

Gaultiere expose hidden subconscious perceptions of God as threatening, intimidating, manipulative, or just uncaring. These negative perceptions can block you from knowing God's love for you. You don't have to block God's love anymore! Read how you can unlock powerfully positive perceptions of the God of love in your life.

In the pages that follow, you'll discover positive growth principles that really work. You'll gain the courage to face your life's troubles and tragedies and bring them straight to the loving arms of God. Now that's possibility-thinking faith! Daring to believe from the depths of despair, "It's possible! God loves me!"

I invite you to allow God to use this book to reveal the beauty of His love to you or to a loved one.

Robert H. Schuller

Preface

Mistaken Identity is a book about the hidden hurts and secret scars people experience in their relationship with God. It's a book about quiet questions of "Why God . . . ?" and fleeting doubts of "Does God really . . . ?" It's a book about uncovering and clarifying the distorted images of God that create emotional and spiritual distress. It's a book about how to focus your image of God in His love. It's a book that has needed to be written for a long time. If you desire a deeper experience of God's love, or if you're a counselor, pastor, or lay minister who desires to help people know God as He really is, then *Mistaken Identity* is a book for you.

Probably you or someone you know has at some time felt distant from God, disappointed by God, unsure of whether God really cares, hesitant to completely trust God, threatened by God, pressured to please God, or even angry at God. Uncomfortable feelings like these tend to be kept hidden. It seems wrong to have "negative" feelings toward God. Yet, misunderstanding, conflict, and pain are inevitable in any relationship, especially one with an invisible God. It's time to be honest about these feelings in order to uncover and clarify the distorted images of God that cause them.

We've found that it's common for people who believe God

loves them to struggle to really experience His love in certain areas of their lives. They experience God as being like people from their past who have hurt them in some way. The result is a mistaken identity of what God is really like. Their image of God gets distorted into a Statue God, Marshmallow God, Party Pooper God, Critical Scrooge God, Demanding Drill Sergeant God, Unjust Dictator God, or one of the other negative caricatures of God that we describe.

We've designed *Mistaken Identity* for individual or group study. Each chapter has a "Questions for Reflection and Discussion" section to help you interact with the material. And to help people identify their own image of God, we've created a short survey, the "God Image Questionnaire," which is easy to score and is ideal for use in groups, in counseling, or in personal study. Also included are figures, charts, and case studies to illustrate important points.

This book emerged from Bill's doctoral research, our previous ministry as college pastors, the seminars we've done on related subjects, and our individual practices as psychotherapists. We're indebted to the many people who have shared their personal and spiritual struggles with us. We've changed their stories in order to share their distressful images of God with you.

If you have a story of your own to tell us, we'd love to hear from you. Write us personally and tell us how *Mistaken Identity* has impacted your life and your relationship with God.

Bill and Kristi Gaultiere
South Coast Psychological Center
14150 Culver Dr., Suite 203
Irvine, CA 92714

Mistaken Identity

1 What Is Your Image of God?

That our idea of God corresponds as nearly as possible to the true being of God is of immense importance to us.

A. W. TOZER

Jan rushed into the office and fell on the couch. Pressing herself into the corner of the couch, she grabbed a box of Kleenex. She gave me a desperate glance and then the tears began to flow before she could even say a word.

There was a momentary silence, then the words came pouring out even faster than the tears had just a moment before. "I've tried," she cried, as she held a tissue against her face.

"I seem to continually find myself in crises; I just can't deal with life anymore. I need to get away! My husband has been out of work and last night my son came home drunk. What next? I feel like my life is falling apart. The bills are piling up and we might have to move. Meanwhile, I still don't know what I want to do with my life. It's time for me to be more than a housewife and a mother. I've been supporting the home for almost twenty years. Now I need to do something more with my life. Just when I was ready to step out it was like the walls of our house started caving in on me and now I'm trapped!

"I've tried to talk to my husband about how I feel and he doesn't understand. Even my friends don't seem to understand. They're happy staying at home. Do you understand? What am I going to do?"

As I listened to Jan drowning in a sea of confusion, feeling that she had no one to turn to, I wondered if she felt she could turn to God for help. So I asked her.

"I don't think He cares about me!" she blurted out. She began to rip apart the piece of Kleenex in her hand into tiny pieces as she told me how she had prayed and prayed seeking God's help, but it seemed to her that her prayers just bounced off the ceiling. Nothing ever changed. Again and again she found herself crying out in desperation, "Why won't God help me and show me what to do? Why did He let this happen to me?"

Watching her viciously rip apart yet another tissue, I remarked, "It sounds to me like you're angry at God and feel that He's really let you down."

"Oh, no!" she retorted. "I couldn't get angry at God! Who am I, to stand up and complain to Him? I'd really be in trouble then! It's just that God seems so distant from me. Sometimes I wonder if He even cares about how I feel. But, I'm sure it's just me. I just have to get through this."

After Jan left my office, I sat motionless, sadly gazing at the pile of shredded Kleenex left on my couch. In my heart I still felt some of her pain at feeling neglected and abandoned by God in a time of distress. I also felt God's sorrow at being misunderstood. I kept wishing, *If only Jan could really feel God's love for her*.

Before Jan could truly receive God's loving care and direction, she needed to realize that deep down she felt hurt and was angry at God for not caring about her problems. She didn't want to admit this though because she was afraid it was wrong for her to question God's love for her. What Jan needed to see was that underneath her negative feelings was a cruel image of a statuelike God who stood back from her with His arms folded and wouldn't move to help her even if she was desperate. She felt as if God didn't consider her important enough to take an active role in her life. Instead He just stood and watched her suffer while her life fell apart. With such a distorted perception of God it's no wonder that she began to lose hope that God would help her family through their difficulty and guide her through her time of transition.

Jan's discovery that her feelings of despair were connected with how she viewed God was a surprise to her. She had separated her spiritual life from her emotional life. With her negative feelings toward God hidden, her communication with Him was stopped up like a clogged pipe. Getting unclogged was a matter of allowing herself to express her feelings of not being loved by God to God Himself. This, of course, is just what she was avoiding! Yet, it was the only way for her to reconnect emotionally with God and receive His comfort and strength in the midst of her despair. When Jan became honest with God about her feelings she started to gain a new image of God as the Lover of her soul. For in reality God did care about her situation and was with her in the midst of her pain, desiring to have an active role in helping her to freedom and growth.

Struggling to Feel God's Love

In one way Jan isn't unlike many people we know. In fact, you can probably understand Jan's struggle to feel God actively helping and loving her. Think back to one of your own times of personal difficulty or emotional upheaval. Perhaps at such times you've secretly asked, "Why doesn't God help me? How could He have let that happen to me?" Sometimes you reach out for God and feel as if you get no response. Usually it's in these times of distress that our subconscious attitudes toward God surface. And feeling removed from God's love only makes any other difficulties you face in life worse!

Struggles to see God as He is and experience His love are related to many common problems we all face in life. You know this is true if, like Jan, dark clouds of despair sometimes cover your life and shut out the light of God's love from you. Or you may struggle with feelings of inadequacy and a belittling self-esteem, only to find that at times you feel God is disappointed in you. If you have perfectionistic tendencies and push yourself harder and harder to excel, then it's likely that God often seems demanding and never quite satisfied with you. If you tend to have trouble fully trusting people, you might find that it's even hard to submit yourself completely into God's hands. Or maybe you carry scars from your past and feel hurt and angry that God let those things happen to you.

Whatever your struggles or concerns might be, the chances are good that they are related to whether or not you have an emotionally based concept of God as perfectly loving toward you. We've found that an important step in helping people overcome their personal and spiritual difficulties is to help them discover new and loving images of God that will heal them of the distressful effects of their old and unloving images of God.

In fact, most of the problems Kristi and I deal with as psychotherapists seem to be related to distorted images of an unloving God. A young man asked, "God isn't really concerned about which job is best for me, is He? God must have more important things to do than to take the time to help me with such a small matter." Because this young man felt he couldn't trust God to respond to his prayers and guide him in his decisions, he wasted hours worrying over which job to take. Instead of receiving God's loving guidance, he anxiously fought within himself trying to make an important decision on his own without God's help.

To one businesswoman who was struggling to feel God's love, it seemed that no matter how hard she tried, she couldn't be good enough for God. "I feel like the worm and wretched sinner that God says I am!" she moaned. She was doing everything she could to earn the acceptance of a God who was as much of an unpleasable tyrant as her boss. Feeling so condemned and put down by God, it's no surprise that she had such a low view of herself and was ready to give up her faith.

"But God isn't like that!" you say. "I know He isn't harsh

and legalistic. He's good and loving." You're right. And believe it or not, each of these people knew that too. Intellectually they knew that God was loving, but emotionally they weren't experiencing His love. The young man felt God was passively distant and the businesswoman felt He was overly demanding. It wasn't their doctrinal beliefs that were causing them problems. It was their negative image of God on a feeling level.

We all experience this tension between our spiritual beliefs and our real-life experiences, don't we? Spiritually, you believe that God loves you, but sometimes your experience tells you that He doesn't really care or He wouldn't have let that terrible thing happen to you. It's when we're in difficult situations that we most need to feel God's love. Yet, our tendency in those situations is to explain how we got there in the first place by reasoning that God passively turned His head away from us for a moment and allowed it to happen. How else can we reconcile the existence of a good and loving God and our experience of pain and tragedy? The eyes of faith enable us to do just that—to see God's loving goodness even in the midst of difficulty. When we do struggle to feel God's love it's because of the ugly image of an unloving God that sticks its head out of the mud and stares us in the face. These dirty culprits need to be unearthed and thoroughly washed in the well of living water that our Loving Lord offers us.

But how do you overcome this struggle? What can you do when you have trouble experiencing God's love? Usually people who feel removed from God's love try to shut off their feelings. They just don't let themselves feel. Having negative feelings about God is uncomfortable, so they cling to their beliefs that God really does love them even if they don't feel it.

Instead of hiding their feelings, people need to understand them and work them through with God.

One woman who followed this advice said, "Before I became aware of my distorted God Images, I tried to shut off my bad feelings toward God. I had to accept the fact that I felt anger toward God because it seemed like He let me down and didn't help me. Once I confessed to God how I felt and talked it through with Him I felt free to receive His love for me. Soon I felt close to God again and was filled with love for Him instead of anger."

Our relationship with God is like any other relationship in this sense. When you have hurt or angry feelings toward someone and don't share them you get in trouble. The emotions begin to build to resentment or bitterness and leave you feeling separated and emotionally cut off from that person. It's only when you go to that person and share your feelings that you are able to work them through and get reconciled with God. It's this type of emotional honesty with God that is the only way to get relationally in tune with His love.

What we need to do is get our "spiritual glasses" examined so we don't see double when we look at God. It's like the old story of the father and his double-seeing son.

> A father said to his double-seeing son, "Son, you see two instead of one." "How can that be?" the boy replied. "If I were, there would seem to be four moons up there in place of two."[1]

In the same way, some people have a double image of God. In their heads they see and believe in a God of love, but in their hearts they see and feel a God who doesn't completely love them. It's their heartfelt image of God that most impacts their daily lives.

In the seminar we hold on healing distorted perceptions of God we ask people how their negative God Images make them feel. See if you can identify with some of their feelings:

- "It isn't fair that God allows bad things to happen to me."
- "I feel that God is so distant from me."
- "I'm afraid to ask God for what I really want."
- "God lets me suffer and doesn't come to help me."
- "It seems as if God is waiting around the corner to trip me up. He's out to get me!"
- "It seems that God is never satisfied with my efforts to please Him."
- "I feel so bad about myself. God can't see any value in me."
- "God must be mad at me. He seems to enjoy punishing me."

- "I don't want to pray to God anymore because He doesn't answer my prayers anyway."
- "God doesn't seem to really care about me and my problems."

Becoming Aware of Your Image of God

So what will you get out of it? How will it benefit you to become aware of your distorted God Images? The most important thing is you'll begin to emotionally grasp God's love for you deep in your heart. Instead of "seeing double," your emotional image of God will come closer to matching your intellectual image of God as a good God. Then the God of your heart and the God of your head will be one and the same. When people overcome their negative images of God and really discover God's love their whole outlook on life improves. They start to see themselves as beloved children of God in Christ and are free to better love and serve others.

What we're talking about is a healing process that begins with becoming aware of negative distortions in your image of God. Once you accept the troubling feelings and attitudes you have toward God you can express them to Him and be opened to receive His love for you in a new and deeper way. One woman who worked through this process said, "I feel so secure now, like God really is always with me." Another woman exclaimed, "For the first time I feel that God believes in me and really accepts me!" A young man said, "Developing a good God Image has helped me to finally see the purpose and meaning that God has for my life."

You may be wondering, *Just what is a "God Image" anyway?* Your God Image is the collection of emotional images of God that you have deep inside your heart. It's your private experience of relating to God. You might think of your God Image as your perception of God's attitudes toward you or the way that you feel He relates with you. These perceptions form a certain set of expectations about how God will treat you. I often tell people that their God Images are the pictures of God they draw inside their hearts with the different colored crayons of their emotions.

Others use different terms to refer to what I call the God Image.

David Seamands uses the common term, "concept of God" to describe the way we conceive of God on an emotional level, or our "feltness" of what God is really like.[2] One psychologist uses the term "God-pictures" to emphasize the importance of pictorial symbols and images to spiritual life and language in general.[3] Other psychologists refer to the "representation of God," which they identify as a perceptual construct for God that exists as an internal image in our minds.[4] A theologian named Os Guiness describes the God Image as a set of presuppositions about God that are different from beliefs and creeds about God.[5] Each of these definitions of God Images is referring to our emotion laden perceptual image of God, which is not necessarily the same as our professed beliefs about God.

You might reflect for a moment and ask yourself, *What is my image of God like?"* Before you give a memorized answer from your head look within the emotions of your heart. Many people have an image of God that is blurred and ill-defined, kind of a crazy collage of confusing pictures that don't all fit together. To help you identify your own God Image, there is a short survey at the end of this chapter which you can score yourself. It's called the God Image Questionnaire.[6] You'll also find "Questions for Reflection and Discussion" at the end of each chapter which will help you assess your own image of God.

If you're not sure just what your image of God is, then you're not alone. In fact, one woman Kristi talked to said, "I think that right doctrine about God is so important. I believe that God is holy and loving." Like many people, this woman gave an intellectual response, listing God's attributes. When Kristi rephrased her question and asked the women how she experienced God on an emotional level, she was dumbfounded. She was so concerned about her thoughts and intellectual beliefs about God that she wasn't in touch with how she really felt in her relationship with God.

A seminary student who came for counseling said, "I know God is patient with me. I'm just not patient with myself." He talked about how upset he was because he took an extra year to finish his degree. He then proceeded to condemn himself for being a slow learner and not getting better grades. Even though he said he knew God was patient with him, he was concerned that he might have disappointed God by delaying the start of his ministry for a year. He wasn't conscious of his feelings that God was being impatient with him. It wasn't until he became aware of his misperception of God and received God's patient love that he was able to be patient with himself.

This student's testimony illustrates why it is so important to your personal and spiritual well-being that you become aware of the inner pictures and feelings of your own God Image. Only then can you take the necessary steps to improve your image of God and truly experience His love for you. A. W. Tozer describes the process of uncovering your images of God this way:

> Our real idea of God may lie buried under the rubbish of conventional religious notions and may require an intelligent and vigorous search before it is finally unearthed and exposed for what it is. Only after an ordeal of painful self-probing are we likely to discover what we actually believe about God.[7]

For many of us our image of God is like Dorothy and her friends' image of the Wizard of Oz. If you remember, Dorothy was lost in the land of Oz and was homesick for Kansas. The friends she met in the land of Oz also had some problems. The scarecrow needed a brain, the tinman needed a heart, and the lion wanted courage. They had been told that the Wizard of Oz was kind and wonderful and would give them their wishes. Filled with hope, they sang and skipped down the yellow brick road to the Emerald City. When they got there and met the Wizard they were shocked by a horrifying and ugly monster on a huge screen, blowing out smoke and thundering angry threats at them. The four of them trembled in fear before this image of a terrifying wizard.

They had heard that the Wizard of Oz was so kind and wonderful and would help them, yet the wizard they saw on the screen was so mean he cruelly turned them away without offering any help. It wasn't until Toto pulled open the curtain that they saw the real Wizard of Oz wasn't the one up on the screen. He was a kind old man who was gentle and caring.

In the same way you may be relating to a mistaken caricature of God on the screen of your heart. It's not enough for you to think that the One you turn to for help is *supposed* to be loving. You need to feel in your heart that God loves you. Many people cower in fear and back away from God until they're able to see that the Real God isn't the mean figure on the screen but the gentle and kind One behind the curtain.

Many people are starting to become aware of how negative caricatures of God can be a real problem. Recently, we were surprised to read in an interview in *Redbook* magazine (July 1987) that Dolly Parton recognized this as a problem.

> So many people have distorted views about God. They think he's a monster sitting in the sky, an ugly Santa Claus who points a finger and burns little children. But God is not bad—He's all good, all love.

Not long ago Kristi and I had a conversation with Norman Vincent Peale and his wife about the common problem—even for Christians—of having negative caricatures of God. Dr. Peale recalled that the church he attended as a child had a huge picture of an eye painted on the wall of its entry foyer! The eye had a sinister look and a caption underneath which read "God is watching you." Dr. Peale told us how much that scared him as a young boy and that it gave him a negative picture of a mean God who was out to get him.

Indeed, there is such a need in the church today for people to receive healing for their painful perceptions of an unloving God. It seems that in many ways our "emotional maturity is dependent upon our image of God."[8] It's no wonder we have emotional struggles when we worship a God who is more like a critical parent, a perfectionistic boss, or an absent father than a Loving Savior. Such false images of God can't encourage us when we're down or be a listening ear when we need someone to talk to, much less lead us to spiritual and emotional maturity. J. B. Phillips seems to agree. In his book *Your God Is Too Small* he said, "The trouble with many people today is that they have not found a God big enough for modern needs."[9]

As A. W. Tozer concluded:

> The low view of God entertained almost universally among Christians is the cause of a hundred lesser evils eveywhere among us.[10]

Distorted God Images in the Bible

If you look through Scripture you'll see that distorted God Images are not just a modern-day problem. One dramatic example in the New Testament is the story of Saul. He thought he was serving God by persecuting Christians. Then one day the Lord appeared to him as a bright light on the road to Damascus. Saul asked, "Who are you, Lord?" not recognizing God. It was almost as if God was walking down the street toward Saul, bumped into him, knocked him over, and blinded him with the light of His love before Saul realized who God was! When Saul realized God's true identity he became a changed person and took on a new name. Later, as the Apostle Paul, he wrote about the reality of God's perfect love in 1 Corinthians 13, the famous love chapter. Probably speaking from his own experience, Paul noted the difficulty people have in accurately perceiving God's perfect love:

> For we know in part and we prophesy in part. . . . Now we see but a poor reflection; then we shall see face to face. Now I know in part; then I shall know fully, even as I am fully known.
> 1 Corinthians 13:9, 12

Looking into the Old Testament, you'll discover that even before the Apostle Paul's day Job saw only a poor reflection of God's love. Like most of us, he too struggled to see the Real God of love through the dirty glasses of his distorted God Image. The story begins with Job as one of the most righteous and wealthy men in his time. Then one day all he owns is destroyed, most of his family is killed, and he is afflicted with painful boils. The Book of Job plays out the story of how Job's friends blamed Job for his suffering and then Job blamed God. Later in the story we see that Job discovered the Real God of love in the midst of his suffering and was restored to health and prosperity. See if you can identify with some of Job's distressful perceptions of God.

- "Even if I summoned [God] . . . I do not believe he would give me a hearing" (Job 9:16).
- "He would crush me with a storm and multiply my wounds for no reason" (9:17).
- "You write down bitter things against me . . ." (13:26).
- ". . . You destroy [my] hope" (14:19).
- "God assails me and tears me in his anger and gnashes his teeth at me; my opponent fastens on me his piercing eyes"(16:9).
- "All was well with me, but he shattered me . . ." (16:12).
- "God has made me a byword to everyone, a man in whose face people spit" (17:6).
- "God has wronged me . . ." (19:6).
- "He has stripped me of my honor and removed the crown from my head" (19:9).
- "He has alienated my brothers from me; my acquaintances are completely estranged from me" (19:13).
- "I cry out to you, O God, but you do not answer; I stand up, but you merely look at me" (30:20).

How Do Distorted God Images Affect You?

Paul and Job each learned that distorted God Images block out the reality of God's love. In both their cases when God appeared they were surprised, Paul was knocked off his feet and Job was nearly swept up in a whirlwind! You see, the way we expect God to be affects the way we experience Him. For instance, suppose that you were going to the airport to pick up someone whom you had never personally met but had heard a great deal about. You look at each person coming off the plane, but no one fits the image of the person you're looking for. Finally, everyone is off the plane and you can't find the person you're supposed to meet! Then you're paged over the loudspeaker to go to the reservations desk where the person you're to meet is waiting. You're surprised to discover that he was the first one off the plane and walked right past you! You hadn't recognized him because you had a wrong picture in your mind of what he'd look like. So also, many of us miss God when He comes to meet us because we have a distorted picture of what He's like.

Let me briefly introduce you to four people who emotionally missed God because of a mistaken image of what He is like. Keith is a sharp-looking man who dresses impeccably and is extremely well mannered. He explained to me that as the pastor of a successful church he feels he needs to maintain an image of perfection. Keith's image was pretty convincing and at first it was hard to imagine that he had any problems, especially in his perception of God.

Keith said he came for counseling because he was experiencing an excessive amount of anxiety over his sermons. "Each sermon has to be better than the last," he said. "I'm getting so that I spend hours and hours each week trying to improve my message. Sometimes when I'm trying to write I just freeze and can't decide how to best say things." Keith told me he felt guilty because the stress of preparing perfect sermons for his church was so great that he had to cancel church meetings and counseling sessions with church members.

When I asked Keith how his sermon anxiety started he said he had gone to a church growth seminar a few months before and had compared himself with other pastors. He felt that they were serving God better than he was. As Keith shared his struggle, we began to see that down deep he felt God wasn't pleased with him. He felt he had to be perfect to please God. As a pastor, Keith knew intellectually that God was loving and accepting and this is what he shared with his church. Yet, emotionally Keith experienced God as a demanding tyrant who couldn't be pleased, and so he was fighting feelings of anxiety at trying to "measure up" and maintain an image of perfection.

Marie also had a negative God Image. She came in with a self-esteem problem and, like Keith, was not aware that her misperceptions of God were part of her distress. Sounding as if she was at the end of her rope, she said, "I've had it! I just can't handle the kids anymore. And no matter what I do I can't seem to please my husband. I guess I'm just not a very good mother or wife."

Marie's low self-esteem led her to feel that she couldn't please her family or do anything worthwhile. She felt that if she let her family down or did anything unsuccessfully it would prove she was inadequate and a worthless person. So she'd given up even trying.

When asked how her spiritual life was she said, "I spend time reading the Bible and praying to God every day and I'm real active in my church." With a discouraged look she continued, "But it just doesn't seem God is helping me. Sometimes I wonder if God even has a purpose for my life." Clearly, Marie's distorted caricature of God left her feeling bad about herself. She felt God left her alone to manage her out-of-control kids and to please her impossible-to-please husband. And then she felt that God condemned her for failing!

Just by looking at John, anyone could see that he was depressed. His head was hung low and he was shuffling his feet. John was discouraged because the business he tried to start didn't work out. He had all the business skills to make contacts, market the company, and keep the books, but for some reason, it just didn't work out the way he planned. Ever since, John had been sitting around at home afraid to go out and look for another job.

Now John's anger at God was piling up along with his unpaid bills. "Why didn't God bless us as He said He would? God really let us down," he complained. As he talked further, John admitted that since his business failure he had refused to pray for things because he didn't want to be disappointed by God again. He felt as if God left him when he needed Him most and might do it again. John's distorted perception of God caused him to feel God couldn't be trusted because He didn't keep His promises.

Judy also felt that God had let her down. Her problem was that she'd been lonely ever since her boyfriend broke up with her. She had been praying that they'd get married and felt that God was blessing their relationship. Then, all of a sudden, the rug was pulled out from under her and the relationship ended. She wanted so badly to feel loved and to be close to someone, but felt as if God didn't care and had left her all alone. She kept asking herself, *Why won't God help me and give me a husband?*

Judy was so upset with God that she stopped going to church and wasn't having her devotions anymore. "Why should I go out of my way to please God when He's left me all alone?" she asked. Judy's distorted God Image led her to blame God for her loneliness. She saw God as being distant and removed from her life. She felt that He didn't care about her needs for companionship and love.

The personal difficulties of each one of these people were related to their negative God Images. Keith's anxious perfectionism, Marie's low self-esteem, John's depression, and Judy's loneliness were all compounded by distressful views of God. Instead of going to the Loving Lord for help, they were each in their own way avoiding an unloving God who didn't care about what they were going through. This, of course, kept them from knowing God's love. They needed to receive healing for their distressful images of God and gain a new and healthy image of God as a God of love. If, deep in their hearts, they could experience God as being loving, they'd find the strength to overcome their difficulties and achieve the growth they desired.

You probably also have difficulty experiencing God's love sometimes. This is partially due to the way you perceive God. You'll want to become aware of any negative God Images you might have so you can seek healing and overcome the distresses they create. Then you can truly see and experience the Real God of love who "will meet all your needs according to his glorious riches in Christ Jesus" (Philippians 4:19). You can start by completing the Questions for Reflection and Discussion and the God

Image Questionnaire that follow. Then you'll want to look at the next chapter to discover with which of the "false gods" you struggle.

Questions for Reflection and Discussion

1. How do you picture God? Give yourself a simple test. Think back to a time of difficulty. What attitudes and feelings toward God emerged? What does this tell you about your real image of God?

2. If you were to imagine that God were looking at you, what would his facial expression be? Frowning? Puzzled? Blank? Crying? Smiling? Surprised? Proud? Exasperated?

3. On a blank sheet of paper draw a picture of God. Draw your picture of the way you see Him relating to you now in the midst of whatever you're going through. What does this picture express about your relationship with God? Show your picture to a friend and get his or her feedback on it.

4. If you were to picture God's way of relating to you as an animal, what animal would you choose? A gentle dove? Ferocious lion? Hibernating bear? Majestic eagle? Nurturing mother hen? Wise owl? Innocent lamb? Some other animal? How does this animal act toward you? How does this express your perception of the way God relates to you?

5. Take and score the God Image Questionnaire that follows and discuss your results with a friend.

God Image Questionnaire (GIQ)

The following statements reflect feelings that many people experience in their relationship with God. Please respond to each statement by circling *T* for true or *F* for false to indicate how you **feel** in your relationship with God. Be sure to express how you **honestly feel** rather than how you think you **should feel.**

1. T F: I sometimes **feel** that God doesn't have the patience to be personally involved in the details of my life.
2. T F: I sometimes **feel** that God doesn't respond to my prayers in a special and powerful way.
3. T F: I sometimes **feel** that God neglects to give me what I need.
4. T F: I sometimes **feel** that God takes all the credit for my successes and gifts.
5. T F: I sometimes **feel** that God excludes me from things because I'm not good enough for Him.
6. T F: I sometimes **feel** that God may push me to do things I don't want to do if I'm not careful.
7. T F: I sometimes **feel** that God has to be won over by my efforts if He's going to do what I want Him to.
8. T F: I sometimes **feel** that God isn't satisfied with my efforts to please Him and wants me to do still more for Him.
9. T F: I sometimes **feel** that God holds against me my past sins and spiritual failures.
10. T F: I sometimes **feel** that God punishes me for reasons I don't know.
11. T F: I sometimes **feel** that God won't protect me from harm.
12. T F: I sometimes **feel** that God doesn't believe in my abilities to excel at things.
13. T F: I sometimes **feel** that God doesn't have a special plan and purpose for my life.
14. T F: I sometimes **feel** that God lets me down when I really need Him.
15. T F: I sometimes **feel** that God is too busy to be concerned about the little details of my life.
16. T F: I sometimes **feel** that God doesn't intervene in my life to help me with things.

17. T F: I sometimes **feel** that God withholds from me things I want that would be good for me.
18. T F: I sometimes **feel** that God gets all the glory for what I do and doesn't give me any.
19. T F: I sometimes **feel** that God is self-sufficient and doesn't want my help.
20. T F: I sometimes **feel** that God may force me to do something that He wants me to do.
21. T F: I sometimes **feel** that God doesn't bless me unless I benefit Him.
22. T F: I sometimes **feel** that God is upset with me because I haven't met His demands.
23. T F: I sometimes **feel** that God looks down on me because of my past mistakes.
24. T F: I sometimes **feel** that God doesn't reward me when I'm good.
25. T F: I sometimes **feel** that God doesn't warn me when I'm heading for danger.
26. T F: I sometimes **feel** that God doesn't trust me to do important things for Him.
27. T F: I sometimes **feel** that God has little hope that things will work out the way that I want them to.
28. T F: I sometimes **feel** that God breaks His promises to me.

How to Score Your God Image Questionnaire:

The GIQ will tell you which of the fourteen aspects of God's perfect love you have the most difficulty experiencing. Note that there were two questions measuring each aspect of love. Count 1 point for each question to which you responded "True" and record the total for each group in the "Points" column in the table below.

Each aspect of God's love should have a value of 0, 1, or 2 recorded in the "Points" column. Those aspects of God's love with 0 points you probably have little or no difficulty experiencing and those that have 1 point you likely have some difficulty experiencing. If you have 2 points for a row you may have great difficulty experiencing that aspect of God's love, meaning you probably have a distorted God Image. As you read the rest of the book you will learn how to overcome the distorted God Images that keep you from receiving aspects of God's perfect love.

Questions	Aspect of God's Love	Points
1,15	Patient	
2,16	Actively kind	
3,17	Nurturing	
4,18	Exalting/Encouraging	
5,19	Humbly Serving	
6,20	Gentle	
7,21	Unconditional	
8,22	Accepting/Considerate	
9,23	Merciful	
10,24	Fair/Just	
11,25	Protecting	
12,26	Respectful/Affirming	
13,27	Hopeful	
14,28	Steadfast/Dependable	

2
Meeting Fourteen False Gods

If they could see beyond their little inadequate god, and glimpse the reality of God, they might even laugh a little and perhaps weep a little.[1]

J. B. Phillips

Sometimes when people think they're looking up at God it's actually a false god. This false god is not the Loving God of the Bible but an imposter who only pretends to be loving. You learned in the first chapter that the kind of false god we're talking about is not an idol made of wood or gold or some other substance. It is a misperception that causes you to mistake God's true identity. It's as if when you look up at God you put on a pair of dirty glasses that are smudged with your distorted God Images. Thus, instead of seeing the Real God of perfect love you see a twisted and false caricature of God. These false gods are inadequate; they don't meet your needs. They are also destructive because they take the Real God off the throne of your heart.

In my work as a psychotherapist I have found that people may have one or more of fourteen different distorted God Images. Each of these mistaken perceptions of God is common and can be thought of as a distortion of one of the fourteen aspects of God's perfect love described in 1 Corinthians 13:4–7. (These same aspects of God's love are tested in the God Image Questionnaire.) Negative God Images cause people to relate to a false god who masks the Real God of love and gives Him a false identity. These false gods are spiritually lethal to us because we are deceived into thinking that our negative caricature of God is really God. So the One who created us and holds our very lives in His hands seems to reject us or hurt us in some way. If you've ever felt hurt or in some way let down by God you know that there are few things in life more painful! For if you feel unloved by God then whom can you turn to for help and comfort?

To illustrate each of the various false gods, we're going to introduce you to fourteen people who have misperceived God. You'll see that many of these people are not unlike yourself or someone you know. Each person is a modern day Job, struggling in his or her faith to emotionally hold on to the God of love they know intellectually. Despite what they know about God's love, they each have certain distressful emotional experiences in their personal relationship with God. These distressful emotions have developed into negative caricatures of God which distort aspects of His perfect love. Because of their unloving God Images they are unable to receive certain aspects of God's love and have negative images of themselves as unlovable.

Preoccupied Managing Director God

> How long, O Lord? Will you forget me forever? How long will you hide your face from me?
>
> Psalms 13:1

Freida has become used to people forgetting about her and has developed an image of herself as "Forgotten-About Freida." As a child, she felt that neither of her parents had time for her and now she feels her husband is too busy with work to spend time with her. She even imagines that God has forgotten about her in the midst of His busy schedule. Even though she knows better, she feels as if God is no different from other people. "God doesn't really want to be involved in my life," she said. "After all, why would He? I don't have anything to offer Him. Besides, He's got so many other things to worry about. I'm just a bother to Him. When I approach Him it seems He gets impatient with me because I'm always interrupting Him and needing Him for things."

Freida perceives God as a Preoccupied Managing Director who is too busy managing the affairs of the world to give her any personal attention. In her eyes, a God responsible for holding the entire universe together cannot possibly be concerned about a minute speck like her. Freida's Preoccupied Managing Director God seems to her to be too big to give attention to the details of her life. He has responsibility over so many "big" things that he can't give His time and energy to "little" things. Such a God can be likened to "a harassed telephone operator answering callers at a switchboard of superhuman size" or a "Commander-in-Chief who cannot possibly spare the time to attend to the details of His subordinates' lives."[2] Freida's faulty view of God is like the idol Baal who could not respond to Elijah's challenge to send fire from heaven. Even when all the false prophets shouted louder and louder at Baal, he didn't respond. As Elijah said, he was either deep in thought, busy, traveling, or sleeping (1 Kings 18:27).

Actually, Freida's image of God is quite small. She sees God as being unable to be both powerful and loving at the same time. She relates to a false god who doesn't love her enough to give patient and personal attention to every detail of her life. The god she experiences in her heart is not the One who said He knows every hair on her head and guides each step she takes (Luke 12:7; Proverbs 20:24). Instead, she has mistakenly perceived God to be like people who have been impatient with her and uninvolved in her life. Her distorted perception of God has kept her from receiving God's patient concern which could heal the distress she has experienced from people being impatient and unconcerned. Rather than seeing herself as being of supreme significance to God and the people close to her, she is stuck with an image of herself as being "forgotten about."

Statue God

> I cry out to you, O God, but you do not answer; I stand up, but you merely look at me.
>
> Job 30:20

"Loner Larry" has developed the attitude that he has to make it alone in life without any help from anyone else. He learned to take care of himself as a young boy because he was the oldest of a large family of six children. When I asked Larry what made him think he had to handle everything himself he replied, "I don't want to be a burden on people. Nobody wants to worry about my problems and have me cry on his shoulder." Wondering if "nobody" included God, I asked Loner Larry if he felt he could go to God for help.

"God expects me to do things on my own," he replied. "He's already told me how to live in the Bible, and now it's up to me to be obedient. He doesn't want to hear about my struggles." I commented that it must be hard for him to live life on his own without any help and comfort from God. Hearing me say this, his face dropped and his voice became softer as he responded, "Well, sometimes I *do* feel like there is no one for me to turn to. I'm afraid that people don't want to help me—not even God."

Similar to the feelings Job expressed in the quote at the beginning of this section,Larry feels God is like a statue who just stands with His arms folded and looks at him without answering his cries for help. His Statue God is an unmovable and uncompassionate figure who doesn't help him with anything. Just as when Larry was a boy and felt that his parents were too busy with his brothers and sisters to give him the time and attention he wanted, he now feels that God isn't able to actively be involved in his life and give him the attention he desires. To Larry, it's as if God expects him to be able to take care of himself and so He leaves Larry alone. This Statue God is distant, impersonal, and irrelevant. God is seen as if "He is silently sitting in His office, studying the encyclopedia, His door closed with a 'Do Not Disturb' sign on it."[3]

Struggling to serve and obey a Statue God, it's no wonder that Larry maintained a view of himself as Loner Larry who had to handle life on his own. Larry's Statue God treated him just as Larry felt everybody treated him—impersonally and far removed from his needs. This left Larry feeling deprived of the loving-kindness of God who wanted to be close to him and to actively help him live a productive life. Unfortunately, Larry's distorted God Image kept him from receiving the miraculous kind love of God. Larry desperately needed to receive God's love on an emotional level in order to be healed of the hurts he experienced when it seemed other people didn't love him enough to share in his troubles.

Robber God

> I am set apart with the dead . . . cut off from your care. You have put me in the lowest pit. . . . You have taken from me my closest friends. . . .
>
> Psalms 88:5, 6, 8

Pete is a young adult and a new Christian. Pete feels that a lot of the things he works for get taken from him so he works hard to hang on to whatever he gets. Recently this feeling has been reinforced because in the same week he lost his job, his girl friend, and his first-string position on the school basketball team. Feeling heartbroken and angry over all that he lost, Pete began blaming God for what happened. With a spiteful look he remarked to me, "Whenever I get something good God takes it away from me!" I commented to "Possessive Pete" that it seemed he was blaming

God for what he lost. Pete reacted defensively and said, "Oh, I know God loves me. My pastor said that God takes things away from me because they aren't best for me. I guess He has to make sure things don't go too well for me or I might forget about Him. Anyway, when you become a Christian you have to give up all the good and fun things in life, don't you?"

Surprisingly, Pete didn't know that his image of a Robber God who took good things away from him and didn't want him to have a fun time was actually negative and inaccurate. His Robber God appeared to have good intentions because He hid behind the pretense that He took good things away from Pete to help him be a better Christian. In reality, Pete felt deep down that God enjoyed taking away good things from him and Pete resented this. Not wanting to admit that he was angry and resentful toward God, he had "stuffed" those feelings back down inside himself. He had to see that the "God" he was having trouble with was a false god—a "Divine Spoilsport" or "Heavenly Killjoy" who wanted to make sure things didn't go too well for Pete. It was because Pete's Robber God was such a sneaky and deceptive thief that Pete had difficulty recognizing him as a false god.

Pete's Robber God caused him to feel that he had to walk on "spiritual eggshells" for fear that something else would be taken away from him. His subconscious resentment toward his Robber God kept him from wanting to be close to God and spend time with Him in prayer and by reading the Bible. Pete was stuck in his negative feelings and spiritual frustration until he was able to express his feelings toward God and gain a new image of God as a "Giving God" rather than a Robber God. Only the love of the Real God who is a Giving God could comfort Pete in his grief over losing things that were important to him. Once Pete could see this Giving God, he was able to stop being so possessive and trust that God and others wanted him to be happy and to have good things.

Vain Pharisee God

> If I hold my head high, you stalk me like a lion and again display your awesome power against me.
>
> Job 10:16

Stacy feels she always gets stepped on. She tries to be a submissive wife but always ends up feeling that her husband takes advantage of her. Even as a little girl she felt put down by her parents because she wasn't good enough for them. She's become more and more critical of herself and even feels that she *deserves* to be walked on. It's as if she sees herself as "Stepped-on Stacy." Stacy tries hard to be a good Christian by "giving God all the glory" for what she accomplishes and by doing her best to "deny herself and lose her life for Christ." She feels that to "give God all the glory" means she should never think good of herself and that to "deny herself" is to let people take advantage of her. Though Stacy loves God with all her heart, she was misunderstanding Scripture, and rather than being truly humble she was using Scripture to justify a low view of herself.

I wondered if Stacy felt stepped on by God, so I asked her how she felt God related to her. Replying in a matter-of-fact way she said, "God knows I'm worthless and helpless. He wants me to give Him glory by giving Him credit for anything I do that's good and taking the blame for anything I do that's bad."

I remarked to Stepped-on Stacy that she seemed to feel that God had a low view of her and must feel bad about this. Her eyes started to tear up as she mumbled, "I've never felt good about myself. I suppose I just let God step on me like everybody else because its the only way anyone wants to be my friend. I know God is disappointed in me because I'm not good enough for Him."

Stacy had a negative God Image of a Vain Pharisee God who egotistically thumbed his nose at her and pushed her aside. Her Pharisaic God wanted her to put herself down so that he could feel good about himself. This false god is a prideful "Sitting Bull God" who "relaxes in a yoga position on cotton candy clouds, expecting burnt offerings and homage all day."[4] Stacy's image of God is quite a contrast to the God who revealed Himself in Jesus Christ as One willing to "take up the towel" and serve people (John 13:4–8). For Stacy to see her true identity in Christ as a beloved child of God she needed to see that God approved of her as a "new creature in Christ" (*see* 2 Corinthians 5:17) and praised her as "the apple of his eye" (Deuteronomy 32:10). Instead, Stacy's faulty view of a Vain Pharisee God served to reinforce the low self-esteem she had developed as a child. Clearly, she couldn't trust her heart to God when she felt that He thought little of her and stepped on her.

Elitist Aristocrat God

> Why, O Lord, do you reject me and hide your face from me?
> Psalms 88:14

"Excluded Ellen" always feels left out by other people. She wants so badly to feel accepted by others. She told me that when she was in junior high school her father walked out of the house one day and never came back. Now Ellen says that she feels God is just like her father and that He too is never there for her. Like the Psalmist quoted above, she feels that God hides His face from her and has rejected her.

When I asked Ellen to explain her feelings toward God, she said, "I don't feel that God wants me for His child. When my dad left us I tried to turn to God to be my Father but it seemed that God wasn't there for me either. And then at church I couldn't seem to fit in with my youth group and I always left the sermons feeling that God wasn't pleased with me and could never accept me. I guess I feel like the rotten apple God had to throw out of His bunch of holy apples. I'm just not good enough to be accepted by God and His elite crowd."

Ellen's feelings of being excluded and rejected by God made sense to me when I understood that her image of God was of a pridefully pious Elitist Aristocrat God who was head of the exclusive aristocracy. Her perception of God was that He was too good to associate with a "lower-class" person like her and certainly didn't have any need for her. To Ellen it seemed that when she went to God in prayer He'd look the other way and just walk by her. Such a God is a "god for the elite" who associates only with a privileged class of Christians.[5] Excluded Ellen didn't feel she was a part of that privileged class of Christians. She based this feeling on her perceptions that she wasn't accepted by people at church and that God seemed piously removed from her at the time she needed Him most.

Ellen's distorted God Image of an Elitist Aristocrat God acted to perpetuate her feelings of hurt and inadequacy over seeming to always be excluded by those she loved. Her feeling that God was distant from her, impersonal, and even rejecting, blocked her from the healing experience of receiving the accepting love of the Humble God who associates Himself especially with the lowest and least in society (Matthew 18:4). Instead of feeling accepted by her Father God, Ellen felt rejected and put down. Excluded Ellen needed to gain a new image of God as a Humble God who accepted her and wanted to be close to her. Only then could the unconditional and complete acceptance of the Real God heal her of feeling rejected by her father and other people she loved.

Pushy Salesman God

> . . . [God] you destroy man's hope. You overpower him once for all, and he is gone; you change his countenance and send him away.
>
> Job 14:19, 20

Paula feels pushed around in life, particularly by men. When she was twelve years old, she was sexually abused by her mother's boyfriend and as a teenager she continually felt taken advantage of by the guys that she dated. Now she's decided to stay away from men altogether because she always gets hurt and feels violated by them. Recently, "Pushed-Around Paula" became a Christian hoping that she would feel better about herself. Unfortunately, Paula has had trouble relating to God as a Father and to Jesus as a man because she is afraid of being pushed around by God as she has been by men. Her fears have been reinforced by her perception that her pastor has a "pushy manner'' of preaching about being more obedient to God. She feels forced into being a certain type of Christian and afraid that God will overpower and hurt her, so she's been avoiding Him.

Paula said, ''I'm afraid that God will squeeze me into a mold I don't like and force me to do things His way. I'm not going to lie down and let him walk all over me and stomp His feet on me like I'm a doormat! I've been sold on that 'trust me' line before and been hurt. I know that God is supposed to be different, but I feel so much fear and tension when I think about really trying to get close to Him.''

Then, to get a clearer picture of her image of God, I asked her to complete a scene in which God is standing outside the door of her heart and knocking. She responded in an angry tone, ''He keeps pounding and pounding on my door until I open it; then He forces His way in and tries to convince me to trust Him and give Him control of my life.'' Her tone got sadder as she continued, ''Then I start getting the shakes and don't know what to do. He seems to care about me but He's so pushy. Finally, I say okay because I can't say no.''

Pushed-Around Paula's image of God was a distorted caricature of a Pushy Salesman God trying to sell her something she didn't want. She was afraid He'd rudely force her into a mold she didn't like. It comes as no surprise that Paula couldn't trust a Pushy Salesman God who used her like a doormat to wipe the dirt off His feet and then forced open the door to her heart to take charge of her life. Paula desperately needed God's healing love for the trauma she experienced at being abused and to develop a self-identity that said she wasn't eligible to be pushed around by others. Unfortunately, Paula's distorted God Image resulted in her expecting God to be like her mother's boyfriend and the other men who abused her and kept her from turning to God for healing. It wasn't until Paula turned to someone who could help her by sharing the Real God's gentle and healing love with her that she became able to trust others and gained a new image of God and of herself.

Magic Genie God

> Should not your piety be your confidence and your blameless ways your hope?
>
> Job 4:6

"Manipulative Martha" has the same piously self-confident attitude toward God that Job's friend expressed in the quote above. She felt that she had hope of getting what she wanted from God only if she did the right things to please Him. She was a "daddy's girl" as a child and thought she should be her "Heavenly Daddy's girl" now. She got whatever she wanted from her daddy and she wanted to be able to have whatever she wanted from God. In order to get what she wanted from God she'd play "spiritual games" with Him. She felt that if she prayed in a certain way, "claimed" the right Scripture, or had "enough" faith God was obligated to do what she wanted. With a look of entitlement she said to me, "I have the right to have God's blessings because I'm His child. When I claim one of God's promises He's obligated to give it to me. That's just the way it works."

Martha's God Image was of a Magic Genie God who existed for the sole purpose of granting her every wish. To Martha, God was like a genie who would appear out of a bottle and grant her every wish if only she rubbed the bottle right and said all the magic words. "Rubbing" God the right way was her way of getting on His "good side" to get His blessings. Martha would collect her "spiritual brownie points" and her "heavenly atta girls" by doing good things for God in order to earn what she wanted from Him. She was one of those people who put God in a box and "see religion as a contract: They obey certain rules and God will faithfully look after them and their interests . . . even the Gospel is reduced to a formula."[6] Martha's spiritual game playing with God reduced God to a "Heavenly Fire Chief" or a "Cosmic Rescuer." As one writer put it in an article titled "Your God Is Too Middle Sized," her God is a "Divine Patron" who is at hand to bestow blessings when she needs Him and far away when she would rather not be bothered by Him.[7] The bottom line was that Martha subconsciously felt she needed control over God.

What Martha didn't realize was that deep down she felt she wasn't loved by God just for who she was. She only felt loved and accepted by God if she did the right things and "earned" His favor. This left her spiritually frustrated because she often didn't get just what she wanted when she wanted it. She was like a spoiled little child who would throw a tantrum when she didn't get her way from her "Divine Sugar Daddy." This actually kept her from receiving the true blessings of God. Instead of walking in the love, joy, and peace of God she was crawling in feelings of being unloved, unfulfilled, and anxious. Martha needed help in working through the emotions surrounding her distorted God Image in order to gain a new and more mature image of God. Only a vision and an experience of God's unconditional love could make Martha spiritually mature enough to walk side by side with God and feel better about herself and her life.

Demanding Drill Sergeant God

> Has God forgotten to be merciful? Has he in anger withheld his compassion?
>
> Psalms 77:9

"Never-Enough Ned" is an overachiever. He's always trying to achieve more, bigger, and better in order to feel good about himself. His wife calls him a workaholic, but he says he's just "disciplined." Ned is constantly pushing himself to climb to the top of the mountain of life, but each time he reaches the "top" he discovers that it's only a peak and that a higher peak is still ahead. He justifies his life-style by saying that he does his work for God. "God expects my best," he told me, smiling proudly. "I want to put my faith into action and accomplish all that God has called me to do. If I meet all His demands then He'll have a great reward for me." Feeling weary just thinking about how hard Ned worked, I asked him if he gets tired of feeling that he can never do enough to please God. "Yes, I get tired," he said, "but I can't give up or God won't accept me. And if I slow down for a while then I'll just get in a deeper hole and have to make up for it later."

Ned was working like a slave, trying to please an impossible-to-please Demanding Drill Sergeant God. This false god of Ned's constantly barked out orders at him and made sure that Ned kept up the pace and stayed in line. Ned felt that he couldn't do anything good enough for God, just as he couldn't do enough for himself. Ned's Demanding Drill Sergeant God is like the "Pharaoh God" David Seamands identified.

> He is an unpleasable taskmaster who is ever increasing His demands, always upping the ante. Like Pharaoh of old, His commands move from "Make bricks," to "Make more bricks," to "Make bricks without straw." He is the very opposite of the Heavenly Father-God of Jesus. He is more like the horrible godfather of the mafia who always says, "Measure up or else."[8]

Ned's Demanding Drill Sergeant God made him feel inadequate and guilty because he never could "measure up" or be "good enough." Ned suffered spiritually also because he was stuck helplessly trying to earn God's love and favor. He had no experiential understanding of God's free grace that loved him no matter what, never expected too much from him, and always looked on him with compassion and mercy. Instead, Ned didn't feel loved and accepted by God unless he thought he "earned" it, and when he didn't "earn" it Ned felt that God was angry with him and expected him to make up for his past failures. Ned felt guilty whenever he missed a daily "quiet time" with God. Additionally, he was a "ministry-aholic," constantly volunteering time that he didn't have to help out the church or anyone in need. Ned meant well, but his works-oriented religion caused him to feel more and more anxious until he had a nervous breakdown. The tragedy of Ned's situation was that if he could get a glimpse of the Real God of Compassion who is considerate and not demanding then he could stop being so hard on himself. Until Ned could see a new image of God in his heart, he would continue in the same spiritually and emotionally destructive life-style of trying to achieve enough to be accepted by God, others, and himself.

Outtagetcha Police Detective God

> [God] are your days like those of a mortal . . . that you must search out my faults and probe after my sin—though you know that I am not guilty . . .?
>
> Job 10:5–7

As Job expressed above, Carla feels that God is always watching her, searching for her faults so He can condemn her. She feels that God is "out to get her" and so her spiritual life has become one of cautiously tiptoeing around so she won't get caught making a mistake. "Cautious Carla" tries to do everything perfect for God to avoid invoking His wrath. Spiritually she says she feels like she did when she was a little girl and helplessly tried so hard to please her perfectionistic mother. Now she feels that God is the perfectionist she can't quite please. She said, "God seems so legalistic. I feel I have to be perfect for Him to accept me, but I know I can't do it so I just try not to get caught messing up. I guess I feel that if He sees me blow it, He'll be disappointed and never forget what I did. His expectations are so high that I'm bound to mess up somewhere along the line."

Carla's overly cautious and cramped spiritual life was caused by her distorted image of an Outtagetcha Police Detective God. She imagined God disguised in a trench coat and dark glasses, hiding in an alley just ahead to spy on her and catch her doing something wrong. Her false god is a "Gotcha God" who always arrives at the "scene of the crime" just in time to yell, "Gotcha!" and point out her error.[9] He's like a mean Santa Claus who threatens to withhold her Christmas gifts by making a list of her wrongs and checking it twice to see if she was naughty or nice. For people like Cautious Carla this "Resident Policeman" is the still, small voice of their conscience, which they equate with the voice of God.[10] Of course, doing this is dangerous because then God becomes the culprit who constantly makes them feel guilty and unhappy with themselves. Actually, Carla needed to put the responsibility for her struggles not on God, but on her own imperfect conscience that was largely programmed when she was a child by her perfectionistic mother. Carla's feelings of guilt and fear were caused by the false god to whom she attributed the voice of her conscience. She needed to emotionally trade in her Outtagetcha Police Detective God for the Merciful God. This Merciful God wanted to help her do good and even when she did mess up would tear up the list of her wrongs when she asked to be forgiven.

Unjust Dictator God

> My eyes fail, looking for your promise; I say, "When will you comfort me?" . . . How long must your servant wait? When will you punish my persecutors?
>
> Psalms 119:82, 84

Like the Psalmist above, "Ripped-Off Ron" feels he's not being treated justly by God. He's sixty-two years old and ever since he was a boy he has tried to live a good life to please God. Now he has cancer and isn't expected to live much longer. He feels he's being punished by God even though he's lived a good life. Ron is quick to point out that many of his non-Christian friends are still healthy at his age. He thinks back to previous years when he was persecuted and mistreated by people and felt that God wasn't on his side and didn't punish these people for the wrong they'd done him.

Convinced that God isn't fair and is ripping him off, he said, "God isn't fair! It seems He punishes me even when I'm good and then doesn't punish people who aren't good or even do bad to me. I thought God was supposed to be *for* me and not against me because I'm one of His children. It seems like I always get a raw deal from God."

When I told Ron that it sounded as if he felt hurt by God he replied, "Yeah, I feel like He doesn't want to bless me and that He doesn't care enough to stand up for me when I've been mistreated by someone."

It's no wonder Ron felt ripped off and hurt by God! He wasn't relating to the Real God who is fair and loving but to an Unjust Dictator God who punished him with cancer when he was good and let those who weren't good get off scot-free. His false god seemed to be against him instead of for him and just let people mistreat him without intervening and meting out justice. This Unjust Dictator God made Ron feel like a puny little pawn in a heavenly chess game who gets pushed around and then sacrificed to advance more important players. His Unjust Dictator God required that Ron strive to live a good life and then wouldn't reward him. To make things worse, Ron's Unjust Dictator God had the power to mete out justice but just stood by and watched when people wrongly attacked Ron. Ron needed to work through his negative feelings toward God and gain an accurate image of what God is really like. Then he would confidently entrust himself to God's justice, knowing that in the end things would certainly be squared away.

Marshmallow God

> How long, O Lord? Will you forget me forever? . . . How long will my enemy triumph over me?
>
> Psalms 13:1, 2

Denise also feels that she has been victimized by people because God doesn't protect her. To make matters worse, when she feels victimized by someone's criticisms or mistreatment she has a hard time standing up for herself because she believes that God says it would be wrong for her to do so. Consequently, Denise leaves herself open to be taken advantage of, and part of her self-identity is that she feels she is defenseless. To her, God is no different from her own father who never stood up for her or defended her. I asked

"Defenseless Denise" to describe how she felt God related to her.

"God is nice to me, but He doesn't protect me. He tries to stay out of my problems, figuring that if I got myself into a mess I can get myself out. When I'm mistreated He says I should just take it and 'turn the other cheek.' " Her eyes became teary as she continued. "Sometimes I feel really hurt and wish He'd protect me. I feel so vulnerable and helpless."

Denise had a negative caricature of a Marshmallow God who was too weak to protect her or stand up for her when she was being taken advantage of. Her false god was like a nice and soft "Heavenly Bosom" she could escape to but wasn't strong enough to defend her.[11] He was so wishy-washy that there was nothing strong about him. Her Marshmallow God avoided conflict, hid from danger, and expected her to do the same. When Denise felt taken advantage of or hurt she blamed God for not protecting her. She didn't realize that she was projecting onto God the hurts that she experienced from her own absent and passive father. She needed the strong and protecting love of the Real God to stand by her side and give her confidence, but her distorted image of a Marshmallow God kept her from this.

Critical Scrooge God

> God has made me a byword to everyone, a man in whose face people spit. . . . He tears me down on every side till I am gone; he uproots my hope like a tree.
>
> Job 17:6; 19:10

Don has always felt criticized and attacked by his father. Even now, as an adult, Don feels that he can't be good enough. He feels that God is too dissatisfied with him and often cuts him down for not having done something well enough or for not being a good enough Christian.

"God makes me feel like I'm no good and have no reason to believe in myself," Don said. "Sometimes I think He's whispering in my ear, 'You can't do that so don't even try.' I've never believed in myself either, so I guess I can't expect God to.'' Don imagines that God is disappointed in him and doesn't believe Don will ever amount to anything so He isn't willing to commit Himself to helping Don be a success. ''Doubted Don'' feels so terribly inadequate that he is afraid to try to accomplish anything of significance.

Don's distressful perception of God is of a Critical Scrooge God who is insensitive and constantly negative about everyone and everything. His Critical Scrooge God stands over his shoulder watching him work and viciously cuts him down and points out all his mistakes. This Scrooge of a false god is cold and disrespectful toward Don, never uttering words of praise and gratitude for a job well done. Don knows in his head that God really isn't so critical and negative, but sometimes he feels in his heart that God is a Critical Scrooge like his own dad. Don's feelings of inadequacy and self-doubt are only made worse by his distorted God Image. Instead of feeling accepted as adequate by the love of the Real God who believes in and respects him, Don felt criticized and put down by a Critical Scrooge God.

Party-Pooper God

> But now, Lord, what do I look for? . . .
>
> Psalms 39:7

''Hopeless Hal'' was ready to give up. He prayed so hard that his business would work and then it fell through at the last minute. As David expressed in the Psalm quoted above, Hal didn't know where to turn. He felt God had let him down by not helping his new business get off the ground. Ever since his business failure a lot of things have gone wrong for Hal and it seems to him that God has been the One putting a damper on things. In a despairing tone Hal said, ''How can I have hope now? I thought that God was behind me in my business plans, but I guess He didn't care. I feel like God doesn't have any concern about me and my future.''

Hal's caricature of God was of a Party-Pooper God who dropped in on his party only to turn out the lights, stop the music, pop all the balloons, and send everybody home. The Party-Pooper God waits until you've got your hopes up and then pulls the rug out from under your feet by whispering in your ear, "It won't work. You're foolish to hope for that." This false god has no promising plans to offer you and is pessimistic about any of your own future dreams coming true. With a Party-Pooper God like this, it's no wonder Hopeless Hal felt God didn't have a special purpose for his life and had rejected his dreams. Hal desperately needed to see past his false god and see the Real God of hope and possibility. If he could grab hold of the optimistic spirit of God which anticipates and plans good things for His children then he could get back on his feet and make another go of it.

Indian Giver God

> . . . O God, you who have rejected us and no longer go out with our armies.
>
> Psalms 60:10

Darla was heartbroken. Her fiancé, Stan, had just broken off their engagement and left no door open for their future. She felt that the Lord gave her this wonderful man and now He had taken him away from her. This wasn't the first time Darla had been terribly disappointed by someone she loved. She's felt like "Disappointed Darla" ever since her parents divorced when she was a young girl. Now more than ever she is feeling that God has disappointed her too.

She cried, "I feel so alone. God doesn't seem to be with me. It hurts so much to feel rejected by someone I trusted, and God doesn't even care! How could God let me give my heart to Stan if He knew we wouldn't end up getting married? Why did God let my parents get divorced? I don't know how I can trust anyone again including God. It seems like just when I trust someone they leave me."

Darla's feelings of rejection and disappointment were so deep and long-standing that she even brought God into them. Because she felt that everything about her and her life was a disappointment, she perceived that God was like the people in her life who hurt her. Her painful God Image was of an Indian Giver God who gave her a father and then took him away. Darla felt like she did when she was a little girl, only this time it was God doing the divorcing and taking back the love and support that He once gave. This "Heavenly Heartbreaker" often broke his promises and backed away from her during hard times. Darla reached the conclusion that "God is a disappointment," a "Perennial Grievance" who kept letting her down.[12] She felt that whenever she trusted God enough to receive one of His gifts He'd turn around and take it away from her. Darla's Indian Giver God kept her from trusting in the steadfast and dependable love of the Real God that could comfort her in hard times and even heal her of the hurts she experienced when people in her past broke their promises to her and let her down.

Summary of the False Gods

From the cases above you can see that when you have a distorted God Image you're relating to a false god instead of the Real God of love. These false gods are often secretly lodged in our subconscious minds and contribute to much of our personal distress. As secret enemies, they block us from receiving the love of the Real God that could comfort our hurts and encourage us toward personal growth and spiritual maturity. Part of the process of becoming aware of the blurry areas in our own perceptions of God is understanding the source of our distressful perceptions of God.

Perhaps you've been wondering what causes a person to develop a distorted God Image. Each of the above people had difficult experiences with significant people in their lives. In the next chapter we'll look at the effect our relationships with people have on our God Image and examine other reasons why we develop negative images of God.

Questions for Reflection and Discussion

1. Reread the quote by J. B. Phillips that opened chapter 2. Do you agree that false and inadequate images of what God is like are both funny and sad? Why or why not?

2. In your opinion is having a distorted image of God an idol or just a mistaken perception of God? Why?

3. Did you identify with any of the mistaken perceptions of God that the fourteen people you read about had? Find the two or three false gods you struggle with the most. (You might use your results on the God Image Questionnaire to help you. Each of the fourteen false gods respectively, are distortions of the fourteen aspects of God's perfect love as listed in the GIQ Table.)

4. Reread the verses of Scripture from Psalms and Job that begin each of the fourteen sections in chapter 2. Are you surprised that biblical heroes like David and Job struggled with negative images of God? Which of the verses describe feelings that you or someone you know has had?

5. Based on 1 John 4:8, ". . . God is love," read 1 Corinthians 13:4–8 and substitute *God* for *love* so that it reads "God is patient, God is kind, etc." Try to read the passage with your heart and not just your head. Where in the passage do you have the most hesitation in emotionally trusting in the truth of Paul's words? Try this again when you're in a time of difficulty or need.

6. If someone were to go to a Halloween party (perhaps an "All Saints Party") dressed up in a mask and costume to portray your perception of God how would he or she dress? As a king? Policeman? Army sergeant? Philosopher? Bible-thumping preacher? Angel? Shepherd? Goblin? Soldier? Scrooge? Santa Claus? Wise old man? Some other figure? What does your answer say about your image of God?

3
Creating God In Your Parents' Image

Can men make God? The gods they made are not real gods at all.

Jeremiah 16:20 TLB

You're probably familiar with Jeremiah's illustration of the potter and the clay (18:1–6). He indicated that God's work of creating and transforming our lives was like the way in which a potter shaped and molded a piece of clay with his hands as he spun it around on a potter's wheel. If Jeremiah wrote this analogy, how could he believe that "men make God," as he said above? The clay cannot mold the Potter! As ridiculous as this sounds, Jeremiah observed that people do try and "make God" when they worship self-made idols. These idols that people make are not always funny-looking wooden objects. They can also be false perceptions of God. Just as a wooden idol pretends to be the real thing, so our false images of God take the place of the Real God of love on the throne of our hearts. Indeed, there is a sad truth to this rewriting of the creation account: "So man created God in his own image, in the image of man he created Him" (*see* Genesis 1:27).

Why do people develop false images of God in the first place? The main reason is the natural tendency we all have to subconsciously project onto God the unloving characteristics of people we look up to. We imagine God will treat us as others do. Of course we know better! We know that God is perfectly loving. Nonetheless, on an emotional level sometimes God seems to relate to us just as other people have. For some people God may seem like their emotionally distant father, their unpleasable mother, their legalistic church group, or that undependable person they trusted one time too many.

This isn't a comfortable thought, is it? We like to think that we develop our image of God from the Bible and the teachings of our church, not from our relationships—some of which have been painful. It's easier if our God Image is simply based on learning and believing the right things. Yet, intensive clinical studies on the development of peoples' images of God show that it is not so simple. One psychologist found that this spiritual development of the God Image is more of an emotional process than an intellectual one. She brings out the importance of family and other relationships to the development of what she calls one's "private God." She says that, "No child arrives at the 'house of God' without his pet God under his arm."[1] And for some of us the "pet god" we have tied on a leash to our hearts is not very nice, nor is it biblically accurate. This is because our negative images of God are often rooted in our emotional hurts and the destructive patterns of relating to people that we carry with us from our past.

Projected Images of God

Susan's image of God is the "Pushy Salesman God" she fears will overpower her and force her to do things his way. She avoids getting close to God emotionally because she feels that, if she trusts

Him, He'll take advantage of her. When she can counseling she was only vaguely aware that she had s feelings toward God and she simply attributed these f being a "good Christian." Actually, the problem sh me about was that she couldn't get emotionally involved with men without starting to feel hatred and anger toward them. She was almost thirty years old and wanted to settle down and get married but, as she said to me, "Every time I get close to a man those awful feelings come up from nowhere and the relationship falls apart."

When I asked Susan how this started she began crying uncontrollably as she shared something she'd held inside herself for over twenty years. When she was only eight years old she had been molested by an uncle she was staying with while her parents were on vacation. In the course of her counseling we discovered that this traumatic experience led her to avoid emotional closeness with all men in her life. Of course, she was incredibly angry at this uncle who had violated her. She was even more angry at her father for not somehow knowing to protect her from his brother.

To make things worse, Susan's anger over the hurt she'd experienced got projected onto God as well. God became a projected image of her uncle and other men she feared. She couldn't keep from asking, "Why did God let this happen to me?" She didn't know how to relate to God as her "Father in heaven" so she tried to relate to Jesus as her "Friend," but even that troubled her because He was like a "man" to her. Susan knew that God was supposed to be different and was perfectly loving, and this made her want to turn to Him when she was having problems. But knowing in her head that she could trust God to care for her wasn't enough because in her heart she was filled with fear and hesitation. The trauma she experienced when she was eight and the subsequent difficulties she had with men led her to project her distrust onto God. In spite of what she as a Christian "knew" to be true about God, she had an emotionally distressful God Image. Her image of God was rooted in the core of her heart underneath her beliefs and doctrines.

Susan needed to work through her feelings over the issues

surrounding her molestation with someone who could share God's love with her by being there for her emotionally instead of just giving her advice. Only then could she grow to emotionally trust that God wasn't pushy and harsh, but gentle and kind.

Many people like Susan carry emotional wounds from their past which lead them to develop distressful God Images. They end up subconsciously projecting onto God the negative characteristics of the people who hurt them. One young man had been physically abused by his father. A woman had been repeatedly put down in front of her peers by her first-grade teacher. Another woman was viciously teased and ostracized as a teenager. For each of these people, the emotional wreckage from these experiences in their past affected their relationships with others, including God. This is true for you as well. If you carry unhealed wounds from your past they will inevitably have a destructive impact upon your relationship with God. You may start to believe that you are "eligible" to be abused, neglected, put down, or rejected by other people and even God. In such cases, no matter what you believe and know to be true about God intellectually, on an emotional level you are likely to anticipate that God will treat you like the people who hurt you.

The difficulties some people carry from their past are more subtle than being sexually abused like Susan. Jon is an example of someone who developed a distorted image of God not from emotionally traumatic experiences but because of a pattern of difficult interactions with his parents. Jon's father was a hard-working and aggressive man driven to succeed in life. Jon's mother was much more in the background than his father; she was very quiet and emotionally withdrawn and distant. Jon indicated that he had trouble with both his parents.

"I couldn't do enough to please my dad and I never felt close to my mom." Because Jon didn't know anything other than what he had experienced in his relationship with his parents, he projected his attitudes onto God. Thus, he felt he had to earn God's respect by what he did and he felt God was impersonal toward him. Jon's God Image was merely a "parental hangover."[2] His image of a Demanding Drill Sergeant God he could never do enough to please came largely from the pattern of his interactions with his father, while his perception of a Statue God, impersonal and emotionally removed from him, came from his relationship with his mother.

People like Jon get their negative God Images from a series of interactions with significant people in their lives rather than from one or two emotionally traumatic life experiences. Unless they are able to break out of these habitual ways of interacting with people, they develop attitudes toward God based on these interactions. Some people try to follow all the rules to avoid being punished by a legalistic God. Others feel that since they get whatever they want from people, it should be the same with God. Others are convinced that life is not fair so they have to take care of themselves because God won't make things fair. Still other people live by the motto that "when the going gets tough the tough get going," so they think that they shouldn't depend on God for things. Whatever the case, just like those who have experienced emotional trauma, these people develop their distorted God Images from projecting characteristics of other people onto God.

This tendency to project characteristics of people onto God is easily heard in some of the things children say about God. Children have a way of innocently saying and doing funny things in their attempt to understand God, don't they? You may have some of your own stories to add to these:

- A young boy who heard that God was everywhere refused to sit in his favorite chair for fear of "sitting on God and hurting Him."
- One child wondered, "If God is invisible then how come I have to close my eyes to talk to Him?"
- A little girl asked, "Is God bigger than you, Daddy?"
- When talking with his grandpa, one little boy said: "I'm not sure God really hears my prayers. Maybe He has trouble hearing like you do, Grandpa. I wonder if He needs big ears like you do."
- In response to the question "Where do prayers go?" one child said they "floated" up to God on the clouds. Another child

claimed that an invisible microphone carried them up to God. A third child believed that stars carried prayers up to God.[3]

- A young girl asked her mommy: "If God was there before the world was made, what did He walk on?"[4]

How God's Perfect Love Becomes Painful

God's perfect love becomes painful when your God Image is partially made up of projected images of unloving characteristics of parents, relatives, friends, teachers, and others you've looked up to. In such cases, the good news of God's love for you becomes painfully bad news. The God of love becomes the God who "really doesn't care about me." What happens is that God's way of relating to you is misperceived as being similar to the negative way you were treated by others who were supposed to love you. This is especially true if your troubled relationships occurred during your early development years of childhood and adolescence. For when significant people in your life hurt you or relate to you in an unhealthy way you begin to develop unloving attitudes toward yourself and negative expectations as to how others will treat you in the future. This quickly becomes a pattern of self-fulfilling prophecy in which other people treat you the way you feel about yourself and as you expect them to treat you. It isn't long before your relationship with God gets pulled into this vicious cycle and you feel that God doesn't really love you completely either.

The reason other people are so important in the development of your image of God as a God of love is because your relationship with God is one of faith. None of us can physically see, touch, or hear God. So if your faith is to have relevance to your day-to-day experience of life, you need people you can physically interact with to represent and express God's love to you.

> It is the good news of God loving us transmitted to us relationally that has the greatest impact on us, for it meets us in a way that is real to us in our everyday life. Unless the propositional gospel of God loving us as we are in Jesus Christ is translated

relationally in a way that is real to us as individuals, it often falls on deaf ears.[5]

Clearly, to just know intellectually that God loves you isn't enough to sustain you. You need to know emotionally deep in your heart that He loves you by feeling His love expressed to you through people. " 'God is love,' can make no saving sense to a human being who has never known what it is to be loved."[6]

This shouldn't come as a surprise. The Apostle Paul said the same thing using the illustration that we are to be Christ's ambassadors to one another (2 Corinthians 5:20). An ambassador is someone who comes in the name of another to personally represent him. Our nation has ambassadors in many foreign countries to represent our government. God does the same thing! He sends me to you so that in our relationship I am His ambassador of love, sharing His love with you on a daily basis. Carl Barshinger, a Christian psychologist from my hometown of Barrington, Illinois, put it well when he said, "The arms God uses for holding me are yours."[7]

Usually the ambassadors who emotionally represent God to us are our parents or someone else we look up to like a counselor, pastor, teacher, friend, or relative. It's when these ambassadors represent God's love poorly that we are likely to misperceive His way of relating with us. Of course, the most important representatives of God's love are parents. All of us need to have a trust-based and loving relationship with a parent or parental figure in order to emotionally conceive of such a relation with God.[8]

The process of God's perfect love becoming painful is illustrated in the figure on page 62. In the center of the circle is God expressing His perfect love for us according to the fourteen aspects of unfailing love listed by Paul in 1 Corinthians 13:4–7. The next ring of the circle shows that people in our lives who are ambassadors of God may wound us by neglecting to properly love us. In the fourth ring of the circle are our distorted images of God, which we develop from unloving people who poorly represent God's love to us. Finally, the outermost ring of the

HOW PERFECT LOVE BECOMES PAINFUL

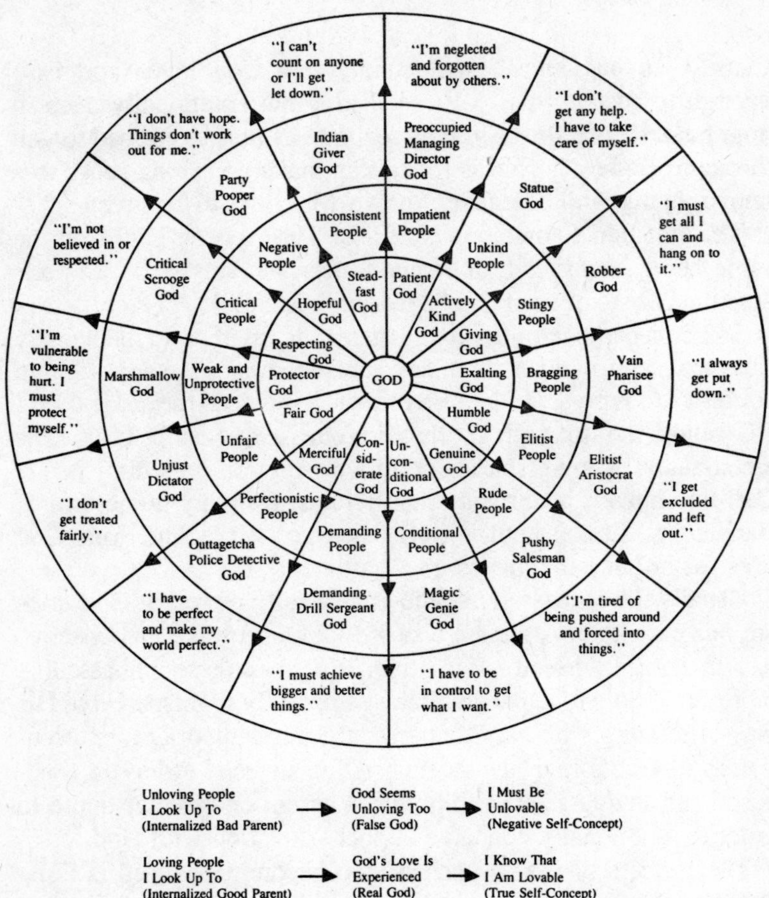

Unloving People I Look Up To (Internalized Bad Parent)	→	God Seems Unloving Too (False God)	→	I Must Be Unlovable (Negative Self-Concept)
Loving People I Look Up To (Internalized Good Parent)	→	God's Love Is Experienced (Real God)	→	I Know That I Am Lovable (True Self-Concept)

circle shows the painful result of this process is that we sta
accept the distressful messages or "life scripts" that seem to bε
given from people and even God. Thus, we feel, "I always get stepped on," "No one really wants to help me with my problems," or, "I'm not worth being respected," and so on.

Another way of looking at why we tend to project unloving characteristics of significant people in our lives onto God is that these people we look up to tend to become "internalized parents" inside us. Because we often try to please and earn the respect of our parents and significant others, the attitudes we perceive they have toward us are easily accepted as truthful and are internalized within us. This internalized parent is made up of the values and attitudes of our significant others and becomes an ego state or frame of mind within us that's constantly judging us. The inner parent that we initially form as children is the psychological foundation upon which we build our God Image and our self-image. If we perceive the significant people in our lives as unloving toward us in some way, it is likely we will subconsciously anticipate that other people and God will treat us the same way.

Is the Voice of Your Conscience the Voice of God?

Some people live with an "inner policeman" constantly policing all they do and barking out orders at them. Others live with a still, small voice constantly whispering guilty condemnations in their ears. Whether the inner voice that tells you what to do is a bark or whisper, you know what I'm talking about. People will try to tell you that these inner voices that cause you to feel guilty and unhappy before, during, or after supposed wrongdoing are actually the voice of God hounding you.

> Yet to make conscience into God is a highly dangerous thing to do. For one thing, conscience is by no means an infallible guide; and for another it is extremely unlikely that we shall ever be moved to worship, love, and serve a nagging inner voice that at worst spoils our pleasure and at best keeps us rather negatively on the path of virtue.[9]

Romans 2:15, Paul separates the voice of con-
inborn moral sense he calls the law written on the
nscience is really a part of the internalized parent
scussed. It comes from your perception of the
of your parents and others who were significant
authorities for you in your formative years.[10] When you mistake the guilt-inducing condemnations of your conscience as the voice of God you develop a distorted God Image.

A young marine corporal related to God as either an Outtagetcha Police Detective God or a Demanding Drill Sergeant God. He felt that he was always failing God's "inspections" and could never perform well enough to please Him. This marine developed a legalistic brand of Christianity that was very works oriented. Because he couldn't "measure up" to the requirements and demands of his critical conscience, he constantly fought an inner feeling of inadequacy and guilt that he mistook as being from God. Like this marine, some people project onto God the negative attitudes that have been programmed into their consciences. If your image of God comes from the voices of your conscience then you probably have developed some negative God Images.

Misinterpreting Scripture

When people read the Bible, they bring with them their own preconceived ideas and beliefs. These tend to influence the way they read and interpret Scripture. Even trained theologians must be careful to stick to the intent of the authors when they interpret the Bible. Many of the Christians that we see for counseling unintentionally misuse certain Scriptures to justify negative images of God and themselves. One girl misused the Bible to reinforce her low self-esteem saying, "God says I'm just a poor, pitiful sinner and that I'm as worthless as a worm or a pile of dust." Not only had this girl misunderstood the true meaning of those Scriptures, but she had also ignored Scriptures that said she was "the apple of God's eye," "the head and not the tail," and "a glorious new creature in Christ" (*see* Psalms 17:8; Deuteronomy 28:13; 2 Corinthians 3:18; 5:17).

A couple I counseled had also allowed a misunderstanding of Scripture to lead to distorted God Images. The wife felt that because God wanted her to be a "submissive wife" she should let herself be a doormat for her abusive husband and not say anything when he mistreated and took advantage of her. She and her husband missed Paul's other advice to "submit to one another" and that husbands were to sacrificially love their wives and give themselves up for their wives, even as Christ did for the church (Ephesians 5:21, 25). In this case the wife felt God wanted her to be a doormat for her husband and had little respect for her as a competent woman. The husband felt God gave him the right to take advantage of her.

A man took Paul's words in Galatians 6:5 that "each one should carry his own load" to mean that he shouldn't need anybody's help with his problems. He was dumbfounded when I pointed out to him that three verses prior to the one he had quoted, Paul had indicated that it is right for people to help one another, saying that people were to "carry each other's burdens." Because of his distorted God Image, this man felt that God would look down on him if he needed other people's help to handle his problems. Like the others, he misunderstood the intended meaning of certain Scriptures and ignored other relevant portions of the Bible so that it was used to confirm inner beliefs and feelings.

Os Ginnis, in his book *In Two Minds,* said such problems of faith are far more than mere problems of intellectual doubt or misinterpretation of Scripture. He compared the ability to have faith in a loving God to the ability of a wounded hand to grasp an object.[11] Picture yourself with a painful, open wound in the palm of your hand. Now imagine that you want to use this hand to grasp an object. You can't do it! Even though your hand is normally strong enough, the wound makes it too painful for you to grasp the object. This is a picture of what it is like for a person with buried emotional wounds to try and emotionally grasp God's love for them. It's so painful to reopen that inner wound! It seems retend it isn't there. Yet, the consequence for not emotional healing for those inner wounds is great. We self-defeating patterns of living, struggling to believe rts that God's love can reach our inner hurts. It seems too good to be true that things could change. So we hang on to the familiar and misinterpret Scripture to confirm our haunting feeling that we really aren't that lovable just as we are.

Ineffective Religious Teaching

Another source of distorted God Images is poor religious teaching and training that we sometimes receive from pastors and other Christian leaders we look up to. This was the case for Joe, who was raised in a Southern Baptist church. His pastor was a hellfire and brimstone preacher so skilled at arousing guilt in his congregation that every Sunday he was able to get half of the people to come up front for an altar call.

As Joe recalled, "I grew up feeling that everything about me was sinful and that God was always looking to punish me." Joe's God was a harsh and punitive Unjust Dictator God. He developed this negative view of God partly from his church's overemphasis on preaching about God's punishment of sin and underemphasis on God's love and compassion for the sinner. Most of the Christians in Joe's church felt more like worthless sinners rather than priceless and righteous saints. Joe's pastor meant well, but he wasn't effective in helping the people in his church realize their glorious identity as new creatures in Christ.

Because Christian ministers—whether they be pastors, counselors, or other leaders—are clearly in a position of being God's ambassadors to us, they have tremendous influence on our perception of God. Kristi and I recently visited a church where the pastor preached a message on how "every defeat in our lives is a deliberate defeat from God to punish us for our sin." We looked at each other in shock as we listened to this pastor twist Scripture to make God out to be a bloodthirsty headhunter on the warpath to kill His enemies! The danger of this sermon is that it's a half-truth.

Some defeat in our lives is due to God disciplining us for our sin, but not all. Since we talk to people every day who are suffering from other people's sin against them or from some tragic circumstance, we couldn't help but think about the people in that church who must have felt they had been slugged by God. What about the woman who is being abused by her husband? The teenager whose parents just got a divorce? The little girl who has been afraid to tell anyone that her father touches her in her private places? The man who just got fired and can't find another job? The widow whose husband recently died? Are these people being punished by God? We could make an endless list of unfortunate people like this who could have been sitting in church with us that morning experiencing "defeat" for reasons other than something sinful they did.

All Christian ministers are certainly not like these two examples. In fact, usually when religious teaching is ineffective it is not as much because of what is said as what is not said. David Seamands, a pastor himself, noted this.

> Many pastors and Christian workers . . . assume if the doctrines and ideas they preach are Biblically correct, they will automatically clear up a person's concept of God and enable him to believe in God and trust Him. They imagine that the Holy Spirit, as it were, somehow drills a hole in the top of the hearer's head and pours the pure truth into him.
>
> With many people, nothing could be further from the truth. For although the Holy Spirit is the One who reveals the truth, what the listener hears and pictures [about God] still has to be filtered through him.[12]

Pastors, priests, and other people helpers need to become aware of the distorted God Images of the people to whom they minister. These negative images of God will cause people to perceptually filter out the good news of God's love. To help those who have distorted God Images, we must reach them on an emotional level. Only then can they receive healing for the past difficulties that caused their negative images of God and gain a new and more positive image of God.

Traumatic Circumstances

Philip Yancey found that Christians who experience intense suffering often find themselves asking the question that was also the title of his book: *Where Is God When It Hurts?*[13] Harold Kushner, in his book *When Bad Things Happen to Good People* asked, "Why do bad things happen to good people?"[14] These authors were looking at a dilemma people have faced for centuries. Even in the Bible we find people struggling in their faith and asking why God allows them to suffer. David asked God, ". . . Why do you hide yourself in times of trouble?" and the sons of Korah cried out to God, "Why do you hide your face and forget our misery and oppression?" (Psalms 10:1; 44:24). And as we mentioned earlier, Job suffered immensely even though he was considered a righteous man. It seemed to him that God not only refused to deliver him from his suffering, but also seemed to be personally inflicting him with more and more pain. Job cried out to God, "Why do you hide your face and consider me your enemy?"

Many of us in our lifetime also become subject to traumatic circumstances that we cannot explain. Often our tendency is to blame God for what happened to us. This was the case for Eric and Nancy, who lost their teenage son Bobby to a fatal river-rafting accident. With tears running down her cheeks, Nancy told me they usually didn't let Bobby take part in risky adventures but decided that this time it would be okay because his church youth group was sponsoring the trip. Eric said they had trusted the church wouldn't take the kids on a trip that was too dangerous. They were both angry at the church but didn't know who to blame. When it got right down to it, I discovered that they blamed God. Nancy cried, "Why did God let this happen? Why did it have to be my son who died? God could have saved Bobby from hitting his head on that rock!"

This was no time for them to hear pious words that all suffering has a purpose and that God can work even this for good. The only comfort they could find in the midst of the tragedy was that Bobby was in heaven and they'd someday be with him again. Once we had worked through their feelings of loss I surprised

Eric and Nancy by asking them if they had forgiven God. Even though they had been blaming God, they hadn't thought of forgiving Him. Because they felt inside that God had done this to them, they needed for their own sakes to forgive God. Fortunately, as Lewis Smedes pointed out, God is big enough to handle our anger at Him and to let us "forgive" Him.[15]

Did God really take Bobby's life away as it seemed to Eric and Nancy? Without taking away God's sovereignty, we must not lose sight of His being a good and loving God who seeks to give us life, not death. Until Eric and Nancy faced their anger at God and "forgave" Him they couldn't see any goodness and love in God at all. Of course, even after they forgave God they still had unanswered questions, but at least they were able to reconnect with God and put the pieces of their lives back together. They were able to discard their perception of God as an Indian Giver God who gave Bobby to them and then took him away.

Many people like Eric and Nancy go through traumatic experiences that cause them to blame God and develop a distorted God Image. Few people are willing to face their anger at God and work through it as this couple did. People who never get out of the blaming God stage stay spiritually stuck in the pain of their distorted God Images like a fly caught on a piece of flypaper.

Effects of Distorted God Images on Personality

We've seen that we all fight the tendency to "make God" in the image of people with whom we've had interpersonal difficulties. We also develop distorted God Images from our harsh consciences, misunderstanding of Scripture, ineffective religious teaching, and blaming God when bad things happen to us. Now let's look briefly at what goes on inside us when we "create God in our own image." The critical question here is How are the aspects of our personality involved in our acquiring a negative picture of God?

We might consider that there are five parts of our personality—we perceive, want, feel, think, and do. The Bible tends to refer to these five aspects in a metaphorical way, using parts of our physical bodies to represent these inner ways of functioning.

Often, the Bible will use the eyes to refer to our perceiving, the stomach to represent our desires, the heart to represent our feelings, the brain or mind to speak of thinking, and the feet or walking to refer to doing.

In the diagram on page 71 we've illustrated what goes on inside people who have distressful God Images. We've put the diagram on a wheel to show the general direction the development of a negative caricature of God might take. The first stage in the development of distorted God Images is the precipitating circumstance. This represents the sources of difficulty that we've talked about in this chapter, the most common of these being interpersonal injuries. The second stage represents the actual picture or perception of God that we see when we look at God "through" the people who have hurt us and thus been poor ambassadors (representatives of God).

In the third stage is our empty stomach, which indicates our hunger or unmet need for God's perfect love. Fourth in the development of our distorted God Images we dwell on negative thoughts about God not really loving someone as "unlovable as me" (examples of these negative thoughts are listed in the outtermost ring of the diagram: "How Perfect Love Becomes Painful," page 62). In the fifth stage, we've shown a broken heart that experiences distressful feelings over imagining that God is like the people who have hurt us. The sixth aspect is our doing, which often is some sort of emotional distancing of ourselves from God. Last is the resulting situation or outcome in which we are separated from experiencing God's perfect love and thus fall short of our potential as Christians.

We will look at this seven-stage process again in chapter 9 when we go over specific things we can do at each stage to reverse the direction of the destructive wheel of our distorted God Images. So far in our journey together we've learned what distressful God Images are, seen fourteen false gods, and gained insight into why we develop them. Now it's time to look closely at some of the effects negative God Images have on our personal and spiritual well-being.

THE IMPACT OF DISTORTED GOD IMAGES ON PERSONALITY

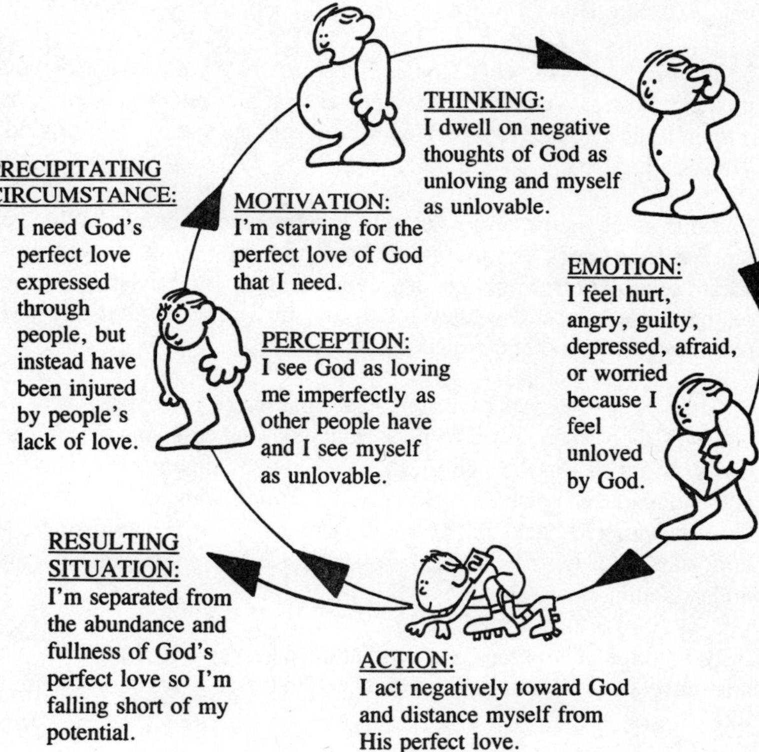

Questions for Reflection and Discussion

1. What is your reaction to the idea that we "create" God in our own image, seeing Him as like ourselves or others? Is this inevitable?

2. Is your image of what God is like most like your image of your mother, father, yourself, or someone else? Who has been most influential in helping you develop a biblically accurate image of God? Who has hindered you in this?

3. Look at the figure "How Perfect Love Becomes Painful." Which of the "self-messages" in the outermost ring of the circle do you most identify with? Follow the messages you identify with toward the center of the circle to see how they relate to your image of God and your relationships with others.

4. Do you agree that the voice of your conscience isn't necessarily the voice of God? Whose voice does your conscience sound like? Your dad's? Mom's? Boss's? Minister's? Your own? Someone else's? What is the tone of that voice like? Soft? Loud? Intimidating and threatening? Guilt inducing? Legalistic? Lenient? Demanding? Perfectionistic? Certain, sure, and rigid? Flexible and open-minded? Loving, gracious, and understanding?

5. What type of religious teaching have you received? How does your answer relate to your answer about what the voice of your conscience is like?

6. Refer back to the figure at the end of chapter 3 titled "The Impact of Distorted God Images on Personality." Based on your knowledge of the negative God Images you struggle with answer the following questions: What needs do your negative God Images leave unfulfilled? (For example, needs for love, understanding, belonging, security, esteem, purpose, joy, etc.) What negative thoughts about God do you catch yourself dwelling on in times of difficulty? What emotions do your negative God Images conjure up in you? How does your image of God affect your devotional life?

4 When Will God Wipe Away My Tears?

. . . You have collected all my tears and preserved them in your bottle! You have recorded every one in your book.

Psalms 56:8 TLB

How touching David's words are. It's comforting to think that each tear and each sad thought we have is held dear to God's heart. For some of us though, it almost sounds too good to be true, doesn't it? Our tears seem too many to collect and record, our pain too great to be comforted. One woman cried out, "Where was God when my husband died, leaving me to take care of three small children?" An adolescent boy gave me a callous, hard look and said, "All I've known is chaos and fighting. How can I trust that God really loves me when He gave me an alcoholic father and a mother too busy to worry about me?" A hardworking farmer, who was a committed Christian, shared with me his tragedy of having his farm totally destroyed by a flood: "All that I've worked so hard for has been taken away from me. My life savings is wiped out. What did I do to deserve this from the hand of the Almighty?"

What could I say to these people? They were drowning in a sea of sadness. If God's arm *was* reaching out to save them, it seemed that it wasn't long enough.

Perhaps you can recall times of distress in your own life when your tears seemed to be unanswered by God. If so, then you understand that dealing with emotional pain can be a long and lonely battle for even the best Christians. When it's our turn to fight, it's no wonder we look at God with pleading eyes of desperation and ask, "What's going on, God? Why? Why me? When will this stop?"

In times of emotional pain our tendency is to question God. After all, if God is truly sovereign then He either causes or allows us to suffer. But how do we reconcile this with His loving goodness? This is not an easy issue for us to resolve. Most of us try to avoid it. We say, "Oh, I don't have any right to question God. It's not right for me to doubt His love."

So the inevitable doubts and questions that our faith must face get hidden underneath our pat answers about suffering and sadness. We dare not let others or even ourselves see that we have these secret questions about God's love, lest God slap us in the face! Actually we're the ones slapping God by not trusting His love for us enough to be emotionally honest with Him. Of course we struggle with doubts and negative feelings toward God in times of difficulty. So many of the heroes of our faith did—David, Solomon, Jeremiah, and Job immediately come to mind. To say that we don't have such spiritual and emotional struggles is to have an image of a puny and pampered God. Such shrunken images of a God that we can't emotionally wrestle with act like a tight collar on our faith.[1] True faith perseveres in difficulty by being emotionally honest with God. Surely God is big enough to graciously help us through the tearful doubts and questions that our faith must inevitably face in times of suffering.

Part of the problem is that in times of suffering and emotional pain we don't see clearly. It's hard to see that God is with us in our tears. Picture yourself crying, your tears sliding down your cheeks and landing in a puddle below. You look down into your pool of tears for the reflection that God is with you, but each teardrop creates another ripple in the puddle. God's reflection gets more and more blurred until it seems that He isn't even there or doesn't even care. Peter warned us in his first epistle that in times of suffering our faith would be tested because we wouldn't always see and feel God with us (1 Peter 1:6–9).

In response to the question, "Where is God when I'm hurting?" one writer confronts head-on the distorted God Images we struggle with when in pain.

> Does our God reach down, slightly twist the wheels of school buses, and watch them carom through guardrails? Does He draw a red pencil line through a map of Indiana to plan the exact path a tornado should take? There, hit that house, kill that six-year-old, but hop up and skip this next house. Does God jostle the earth, playing with tidal waves, earthquake tremors, and hurricanes . . . squashing men out like cigarette butts? Is that how He rewards and punishes, us, His helpless victims?
>
> If God is truly in charge, somehow connected to all the world's suffering, why is He so capricious, unfair? Is He the cosmic Sadist who delights in watching us squirm?[2]

No doubt such images of God as some sort of "Cosmic Sadist" who inflicts pain on those He loves, or at least stands by and watches them suffer, are linked with much of our sorrow.

Christians Shouldn't Have Problems!

"But, wait a minute!" some would say. "Christians aren't supposed to be depressed or have problems! They're supposed to grin and bear it when they're in pain." One woman was told this as a little girl. Now in her adulthood, she is still compelled to force a smile in the midst of difficulty. Despite the tragedies that have befallen her—incest, divorce, death of her little girl—she maintains a smile plastered on her face and tries to bear her pain quietly without letting anyone know.

"I don't want to burden anyone with my problems. God will sustain me," she says in a heroic spirit. Meanwhile, she suffers in silence and alone, her inner wounds like festering sores that are threatening to infect the rest of her body. Though her pain is hidden from most people, those who get close enough to her can't miss it. I couldn't miss it. I imagined her as a weary desert traveler, carrying a huge load of stuff on her shoulders and looking for water. When she encountered someone along the way she'd try to straighten up and smile. She'd only glance at the person's canteen of water, never having the courage to ask for any. What if they refused?

What this woman didn't realize was that by not allowing others to help her she was cutting herself off from the love of God which others could share with her. She was right in saying that God would sustain her, but she missed all the ways that He provided—a shoulder to cry on, a hand to hold, a friend to wipe a tear. She was too scared to open up and share her feelings. *If only God would take away my pain,* she'd say to herself.

When we're in pain it's easy to look for God to magically rescue us. Jesus is our "Savior" and "Deliverer," isn't He? Yet, He never promised us that we wouldn't have pain in this life. In fact, He warned us that people would hate us, we'd have times of sorrow, and we would suffer. This isn't a message most Christians like to hear though. No one wants to suffer.

My friend Ray was no exception. His cry for help was written all over his face and he came to me looking for answers. "I've just lost my job and my parents have been telling me I need to move out and be on my own. Now in addition to finding a place to live, I need a new job! I know I should trust that God will provide these things for me but it's hard to wait. Can you help me?" Ray wanted me to rescue him, but I knew he had to get through this on his own. I felt I was being mean for not dropping everything in my life just to be his best friend, find him a job, and offer him our guest bedroom to stay in. After listening to him for what seemed like hours, I felt like a balloon that had had all its air slowly sucked out of it. Ray was just looking for someone to hang on to and cling to. He related to God in the same way that he related to me. God became like a "Divine Paramedic" who was to be his "Ultimate Rescuer" and save him from life's difficulties. It was as if Ray believed he deserved to be pampered by God.

Ben also thought that Christians shouldn't have problems. His way of living wasn't to grin and bear it, nor was it to find someone to rescue him. Rather than suffering in silence or making others suffer under the burden of rescuing him, Ben went full force into his problems. He was convinced that any problems he had were a sign of his inadequacy as a Christian. Problems were like a red flag, and he was as determined as a stubborn bull to run headfirst into them.

Ben's friends said that he was just "a chip off the old block" because he was so much like his father. His father always told him, "Son, don't complain about things, just grit your teeth and grind it out." Ben took his father quite literally, as he held the stresses of his life in his jaw. His doctor had referred him to me for therapy because he ground and gnashed his teeth so much he was destroying his jaw.

Ben's refusal to give himself permission to have any difficulties in life took a bite out of his spiritual life. His life was so burdensome because of all the problems he had to overcome that he had no understanding of what it meant to "rest in the Lord" or experience His peace. Instead of joyously celebrating in God's grace, Ben groveled in depression, muttering to himself that it wasn't easy trying to live the Christian life in a world full of problems.

Can We Be Devoutly Depressed or Spiritually Sad?

Is it okay for Christians to have problems? When we're having trouble are we supposed to "grin and bear it"? Maybe we can just wait for God to rescue us? Or should we "grit our teeth and grind it out" ourselves?

It's a common spiritual neurosis in the church today for Christians to feel that they're not "good Christians" if they get depressed or have problems. It's as if they have to be models of togetherness—in control, happy, always kind. Consequently, when they meet other Christians who have emotional struggles they distance themselves. "Their faith just isn't strong enough." "Doesn't he know that the joy of the Lord is his strength?" "The Bible says we can do all things through Christ, I wonder what her problem is." And if they have a hard day themselves, or worse yet are befallen by some tragedy, they deny themselves the right to feel any pain or sadness. They act as if everything is okay. We've all met someone like this. Maybe you've felt this way yourself. So, what is emotional pain all about anyway? Is there a biblical way to handle depression and sadness?

Many of the heroes of our faith recorded in Scripture struggled with sorrow at various times in their lives. King David, the one called a man after God's own heart, wrote of many of his sorrows in the Psalms. David's son Solomon was known for his wisdom and great wealth, yet in spite of his successes, his depression and despair fill the pages of Ecclesiastes. Jeremiah was known as the "weeping prophet" and the Book of Lamentations was named so in honor of his tears. Jonah, another prophet, was so distraught that he wanted to take his life. Of course, who can forget Job. His life was filled with anguish during his time of suffering. In the New Testament, the Apostle Paul suffered numerous tragedies and sorrows and, in spite of it all, concluded that in the midst of tremendous hardships and times of weaknesses the loving grace of Christ is sufficient (2 Corinthians 12:7–10).

Our Lord Jesus Himself felt such intense sadness and distress at Gethsemane, just prior to His crucifixion, that the gospel of Mark referred to His sad feelings as "sorrow to the point of death." In each case, these men accepted their troublesome feelings, overcame them by surrendering their human will to the divine, and endured in faith. Their faith was a Hebrews 11 type of faith that perseveres in the midst of difficulty rather than seeking to escape such difficulty because "Christians shouldn't have problems."

A mature and enduring faith in God gives Christians the strength to face sorrow and distress. Troublesome feelings are accepted so that they can be understood and worked through. The sources of sorrow are many—emotional injury, rejection, loss of something or someone important, or loneliness. Sometimes our sorrow is someone else's and we're helping to carry their pain out of concern for them. These reasons are important. We ignore the cause of our depression or sadness when we try to "grin and bear it," find a rescuer, or "grit our teeth and grind it out."

Such means of coping may yield temporary relief, but they don't truly heal our pain and answer our needs.

As the prophet Jeremiah said, "You can't heal a wound by saying it's not there . . ." (Jeremiah 6:14 TLB). Instead we need to recognize our emotional pain and bring it to God. Surely we need the loving comfort of God most when in distress. Yet it is in such times of difficulty that we're most likely to alienate ourselves from God by blaming Him for our problems. Instead we need to blame our mistaken images of Him that tell us He doesn't really care or is harshly punishing us.

God Doesn't Really Care!

If you've listened closely to the "feeling sounds" in the secret chambers of your heart you've likely heard a faint echo that occasionally reverberates within those inner walls of your heart: *Does God really care about me?* Aren't there times when we all wonder this? God is invisible and often His love is not felt. Sometimes it seems that when our pain is the greatest and we need God the most we feel His presence the least.

Of course, even in the midst of these difficult times, we can still believe in His love and trust that He is with us, ready to help us, and immensely concerned about us. But, this is no small task. Somewhere inside, we wonder why we don't feel His love at the moment. In the meantime, we must grasp for faith wherever it can be found. If our reach exceeds our grasp then the loving God we reach out for slips out of our hands and we're left clinging to a mistaken image of a God who doesn't really care about us.

In *A Grief Observed,* C. S. Lewis described his struggle to grasp the care of God when it seemed to have slipped out of reach. He found himself alone and inconsolable when his wife died. His grief threw him into a crisis of faith in which he felt cruelly forsaken by God.

> Meanwhile, where is God? . . . Go to Him when your need is desperate, when all other help is vain, and what do you find? A door slammed in your face, and a sound of bolting and double bolting on the inside. After that, silence. You may as well turn away. The longer you wait, the more emphatic the silence will become. There are no lights in the windows. It might be an empty house. Was it ever inhabited? It seemed so once. . . .
>
> Not that I am (I think) in much danger of ceasing to believe in God. The real danger is of coming to believe such dreadful things about Him. The conclusion I dread is not, "So there is no God after all," but, "So this is what God's really like. Deceive yourself no longer."[3]

Lewis walked a tightrope between avoiding the temptation to distort God's loving character and yet expressing his feelings that God had abandoned him. Many people lose their balance and fall into negative images of God. They end up secretly blaming God for their sorrows. Their feelings that God has shut His door on them can take different forms.

Some people knock on the door to the divine sanctuary and encounter the Preoccupied Managing Director God's voice yelling back at them, "Go away! I'm busy now. Get someone else to help you." These words pierce the hearts of those who in desperation have sought the safe communion of being lovingly embraced by their Lord in His sanctuary.

Another group of people knock on the divine sanctuary's door and hear no response at all. Not satisfied that God is truly not there, they look in the window, only to see the image of the Statue God. His arms are folded, His gaze is blank, and His face is emotionless. These people too find no help from God, no comfort for their sorrow.

A third group of people have an equally negative image of a false god. They also become convinced that God doesn't really care about them. They knock and knock on the door to the divine sanctuary until their knuckles are raw, then finally the door is opened, but just the length of the chain. A pious and stuck-up heavenly saint sticks his head into the light, looks over the poor and sorrowful guest, and proclaims, "I'm sorry, but you do not have the appropriate attire on and besides you were not invited by our host." The host is the Elitist Aristocrat God and, like the other false gods, he, too, is distant and offers no comfort for your suffering.

God Always Rains on My Parade!

Tina was celebrating her fifth birthday at Disneyland. She was anxiously looking forward to the electric light parade at the end of the day when all the Disney characters would march out singing and dancing to music and flashing lights. She waited in anticipation, as she held her daddy's hand. Then, just as the parade started, a loud crack of thunder came from the stormy skies that had filled with dark clouds. The rain came pouring down in sheets and everyone ran for shelter. Of course, Tina was quite disappointed and on the way home in the car she asked her parents, "Why did God let it rain on my parade? Didn't He care that it was my birthday?" Her parents didn't know how to answer Tina, except to say, "Someday you'll understand." They had experienced their own feelings of disappointment at God. Tina's father always prayed before making business decisions, yet again and again the good deals passed him by. Tina's mother felt let down by God when her best friend died of cancer at a young age even though she prayed and prayed for her and was sure God would heal her.

Each of us has a little girl or boy like Tina inside us. We have hopes and dreams for own special parades in life. When we commit these precious desires of our hearts to God and our hopes get dashed, it's not uncommon to feel that God has rained on our parade. Such feelings of disappointment and sadness come from negative perceptions of God. We imagine He is a Party-Pooper God who spoils things and kills our joy or that He is the Indian Giver God promising blessing and happiness and then just when we get our hopes up, He dashes our dreams.

Some people have encountered sorrow once too often and they develop a mistaken image of God as a Perennial Grievance:

> [Their] image of God is a kind of blur of disappointment. ''Here,'' they say resentfully and usually with more than a trace of self-pity, ''is the One in whom I trusted, but He let me down.'' The rest of their lives is consequently shadowed by this letdown. Thenceforth there can be no mention of God, church, religion, or even [pastor] without starting the whole process of association with its melancholy conclusion: God is a Disappointment.
>
> The years by no means dim the tragic details of the Prayer that was Unanswered or the Disaster that was Undeserved. . . . It is impossible for [these] people who have persuaded themselves that God has failed, to worship Him in any way but a grudging and perfunctory spirit.[4]

You probably know someone who has felt like this. Maybe you, yourself, have felt let down by God. If so you're not alone. Even Gideon, who was called a ''mighty warrior'' by an angel of the Lord, felt disappointed by God. He cried out, ''If the Lord is with us, why has all this happened to us? Where are all his wonders . . . . the Lord has abandoned us and put us into the hand of [our enemy]'' (Judges 6:13).

Feeling disappointed by God or as if He doesn't really care about you is not abnormal or bad in itself as long as such feelings are understood and prayed through to resolution. The real problem is the deep-seated distorted God Images that can become entrenched in the emotional center of our hearts when we don't understand and appropriately express our feelings. Negative God Images of a distant, uncaring God behind locked doors or of a continually disappointing Perennial Grievance are the source of much sorrow and depression.

Tears of Joy

Is there an end to this sadness? How can you find joy if you feel God is the Divinely Distant One or the Perennial Grievance? If your heart is gripped with sorrow you mustn't stand outside the door to His sanctuary alone in a puddle of tears. Instead, find someone to wait with you—someone who loves you and can comfort you. Allow this person to serve as God's ambassador to represent His love to you. Your companion will help you discover that it wasn't God who was behind locked doors, but you. You were being held hostage by a false image of Him. In your sadness God felt distant and disappointing, yet He stood outside the door of your heart patiently knocking, waiting until you were ready for Him (Revelation 3:20). Indeed, He was collecting your tears in His bottle and recording them in His book (Psalms 56:8). For God wants to comfort us in our sorrow. But for some of us this is not enough! We want Him to take our suffering away completely!

If God were to rescue us from all sadness and protect us from suffering, we would miss out on the essence of being a Christian and of life itself. In Psalm 30 we get a peek at the secret of David's success in dealing with suffering. He felt God had angrily cast him into a deep and dark pit. It seemed to him this pit would be his grave. From within the pit he cried out to God who seemed so unfair, asking God what benefit there could possibly be in this suffering.

Then a miracle happened. God worked David's suffering for David's good, bringing him "up from the grave" and turning his "wailing into dancing." What did David do that enabled him to discover God's joy and freedom? He faced his suffering head-on, expressing his disturbed feelings and troublesome questions to God and crying out for mercy. His spiritual integrity and emotional honesty built a bridge from his sorrow to God's deliverance. This bridge carried him over the violent rapids of the river of negative God Images which threatened to carry him far downstream, away from God's mercy and love.

Accepting our feelings of sorrow and pain is not easy. It wasn't easy for David either. The many Psalms filled with his tears are evidence of how hard David worked at expressing his feelings to God (*see* Psalms 4–6, 13, 22, 30, 39, 55–57, 69, etc.). When we do this—as painful a process as it is—something beautiful takes place. We invite God into our pain and slowly but surely we begin to realize that He has come to share our pain. As we put our faith in Him, He takes us out of our pain, even if only for a moment, and carries us on His wings up into the "heavenly realms" (Ephesians 1:3) where we can gain a bird's eye view of our suffering. From His perspective we begin to see that "our light and momentary troubles are achieving for us an eternal glory that far outweighs them all. So we fix our eyes not on what is seen, but what is unseen. . ." (2 Corinthians 4:17, 18).

With a renewed vision of God as a Loving God, we gaze into the eyes of our ". . . Father of compassion and the God of all comfort, who comforts us in all our troubles, so that we can comfort those in any trouble with the comfort we ourselves have received from God" (2 Corinthians 1:3, 4). What was once evil becomes good when, in response to emotional pain, we cry out to God, receive His comfort, and gain an eternal perspective on life so that we are able to refocus our image of God and allow our sufferings to be used to help others who also suffer.

Our sorrow is not so hard to bear if in the midst of it we can emotionally grasp the God of love who is with us in our pain. We can do this by turning our "Why God?" questions into "Where is God?" questions.

> The answer to this question is certain: He is on the cross, taking to Himself in Christ the pain, agony, and terror of all the suffering in the whole universe. God does not watch us suffer from the security of a painless heaven, where all is bliss and joy. In Jesus He is a man of sorrows, acquainted with grief.[5]

This same point is well illustrated in the story of Elie Wiesel.[6] Wiesel was a fifteen-year-old Jewish boy who endured unspeakable horrors at the Buna and Auschwitz concentration camps. His worst experience, though, was witnessing a twelve-year-old boy savagely punished and killed on a gallows.

Wiesel said the boy had the face of a sad angel—innocent and beautiful and so unlike the gaunt, disfigured faces of most prisoners. The boy didn't belong on the gallows, but there he was. Then, Wiesel says, the chairs were tipped over and his body fiercely jerked. He dangled limply from the ropes, longing to be dead, but still barely alive for another half hour. From behind Wiesel, in the rows of anguished spectators, a man cried out, "Where is God? Where is He now?" Wiesel heard a voice within himself answer the man, *Here He is—He is hanging here on this gallows* . . . .

Unfortunately, as Brand and Yancey note, Wiesel concluded that God's silence proved He was helplessly dead on the gallows, never to live again. Wiesel misunderstood the meaning of "God on the gallows." God indeed was on the gallows, suffering and grieving with this poor Jewish boy, just as twenty centuries prior He had hung on a cross at Calvary. He proved at Calvary that He not only understands pain and death but has shown us the way to life on the other side.

This picture of the suffering Christ "hanging on the gallows" with us in our times of distress shows us the extent of His love for us. For He suffered all the mistreatment and carried all the sorrows of every one of us combined. He even felt abandoned by the Father God, crying out on the cross, ". . . My God, my God, why have you forsaken me?" (Mark 15:34.) Indeed, His *why* embraces all our sorrowful whys,[7] so that our God Image can be renewed and refocused in His love. His loving grace can turn our tears of sadness into tears of joy.

This is what happened for the sinful woman who went to see Jesus when He was eating at the house of a Pharisee named Simon (Luke 7:36–50). She was so grateful for being forgiven for her sin that she washed Jesus' feet with her tears of joy. She even kissed His feet and poured expensive perfume on them. Can you picture yourself bringing your troubles to Jesus' feet as this woman did? I hope you can. Many people picture God as Simon pictured Jesus. God seems too good to be touched with the dirty and ugly pains of their lives. If God seems distant from your pain remember "God on the gallows" and the woman who cried tears of joy at Jesus' feet.

Questions for Reflection and Discussion

1. Read Hosea 6:1–3. What is your reaction to the statement: "God has wounded us, but he will heal us"? Why would a good and loving God "wound" one of His children? Because of sin? discipline? testing? Or maybe you believe that God only "wounds" those who aren't Christians? Or that if a Christian gets "wounded" then the devil did it?

2. How do you picture God when you pray to Him in a time of emotional difficulty? Imagine that you were to call God on the phone to tell Him about your distress. On a feeling level what response might you anticipate? A busy signal? No answer? Wrong number? The phone rings and rings and isn't picked up until the twelfth ring? A bad connection that makes it hard to hear? An answering machine with a recording telling you to leave a message at the beep? Maybe God would answer, but say, "I'm busy at the moment. Can you call back later?" Or maybe God would answer and talk with you, but give you only a few minutes? If the phone rang for a while without being picked up, would you hang up? Can you feel God answering your call and patiently listening to you in your time of difficulty?

3. Here's another exercise to help you see how you picture God in your time of distress. Imagine that you need something from God and He's in the sanctuary. When you approach the sanctuary door what happens?

Endless knocking with no answer? A voice saying, "Try later. God is busy at the moment"? Or, does God's personal angel answer the door and take you to the "waiting room" to wait for God? Maybe God answers the door, but only after your knuckles are raw? Or, do you get tired of knocking and walk away? Try picturing the roles reversed and God seeks you in your time of difficulty, patiently knocking and waiting at the door to your heart. What's your response to God?

4. Read Malachi 3:2, 3 and 1 Peter 1:6–9. What's your reaction to this picture of God as a Refiner and you as a nugget of impure gold that needs to be tested and purified by Him in the furnace of life's afflictions? Try meditating on this picture to help you get God's perspective on whatever trial you're going through.

5. Have you ever noticed in some of the Psalms how emotionally honest David and some of the other Psalmists were with God? What do you think about openly expressing your doubts, fears, frustrations, and sorrows to God? Try expressing some of your troubled feelings to God by writing a Psalm to Him as a prayer.

6. Meditate on Luke 7:36–50. See yourself crying at Jesus' feet, dumping all your sorrows there at his feet. See Jesus comforting you and caring for you.

5 Worming Our Way to God

My God, why have you forsaken me? . . . I am a worm and not a man, scorned and despised . . . . All who see me mock me. . . .

Psalms 22:1, 6, 7

In the children's classic *The Ugly Duckling,* Hans Christian Andersen told the tale of a young swan's struggle to accept himself. The story starts before the baby swan has hatched and his egg gets put into a nest of duck eggs. He's the last egg to hatch, and as soon as he pokes his way out he wants to crawl back in and hide! All the rest of the birds are making fun and staring at him as though there's something wrong with him. Wanting so desperately to belong in the family of ducks that has cast him aside, he follows the mommy when she leads all her little ducks on a swim. Much to the poor swan's dismay, when he looks at his reflection in the water he is shocked to discover that there *is* something wrong with him! He's not a cute little yellow duckling like the others. He is a big ugly gray duckling! The ugly duckling feels so bad about himself, he just wants to die. He doesn't understand why God made him different from all the other little ducks.

The poor ugly duckling was cast aside and put down by everyone he met. He felt so bad about himself because he didn't fit in. He wanted to be like the other ducks, but was too big and ugly. Then one day he found a group of swans swimming in a pond. They looked so beautiful to him. To his surprise, the swans accepted him and thought he was beautiful. When he checked this out by looking a second time at his reflection in the water he didn't seen an ugly duckling like before. This time he saw that he was a beautiful white swan! The story ends with the once unhappy and awkward ugly duckling now happy to be himself—the beautiful and graceful white swan that God created him to be.

Many of us sometimes feel like the ugly duckling. "Why didn't God make me beautiful, smart, or gifted like so and so?" "God must not really love me to treat me like this." "I'm tired of being looked down upon by pious Christians. How can I be good enough for God's elite group?" Maybe you've felt some of these things. Or maybe you've looked at your reflection in the mirror and felt bad about who you are. If you struggle with a negative image of yourself then you may feel angry at God for making you the way He did.

For a long time the ugly duckling was mad at his Creator for making him such a disgraceful duck. But he was really a beautiful white swan in the making. His poor self-image was a misperception of his created purpose. God didn't make him to be a duck, but a swan. In the same way, sometimes we feel like the ugly duckling that has been cast aside as worthless. We don't see a true picture of ourselves. This is because we have a mistaken image of what God is really like and so aren't able to see ourselves through God's gracious eyes. Like the duckling, we need to reexamine our reflection by looking into the mirror of

Scripture. When we do we'll see a new and beautiful picture of ourselves as gloriously redeemed children of God!

Worm Theology

The happy ending to the story of the ugly duckling sounds so nice, doesn't it? Maybe even too good to be true for some of us. One of the reasons many of us identify with the ugly duckling's feelings of inadequacy and rejection is our "worm theology." In some Christian circles people are taught to think of themselves as worms. They're talked down to and preached at as they're told again and again: "You're wretched sinners with evil hearts. You better deny yourself and shape up your Christian walk. You know, you're lucky Christ saw fit to save such miserable souls as you!" If you've ever been on the receiving end of these kinds of oppressive and condemning attitudes then you know what I'm referring to.

One young woman understands. Her already low self-esteem was driven even lower because of this kind of preaching. "I feel like a piece of trash that's been thrown out in God's garbage! I'm told that I'm bad and dirty and that I'll never be good enough. And then I'm supposed to believe that God loves me." A second young woman took her worm theology even further. She not only felt bad about herself, but actively condemned and put herself down. One time she got on her soapbox and told me, "Jesus said that I'm to hate myself and Paul admonished me to not think highly of myself. There's nothing good in me. I'm just a helpless sinner." I wasn't about to knock the security of her soapbox out from under her feet, but I did feel sorry for her. She was misusing Scripture to justify her low self-image and taking pride in herself for doing it!

Does God really treat the first woman like garbage to be discarded and thrown out as worthless? And what about this second woman? She even used Scripture to put herself down! Does God want her to hate herself? With their wormlike self-images, it was as if these two women imagined God as a thoughtless fisherman who stuck them on the end of a hook and threw them into the water as fish bait! Such worm theology is actually a distortion of the teachings of Scripture. Later in the chapter when we make a distinction between the Christian's old and new self we'll clear up the confusion over the paradox of hating and yet accepting yourself.

Perhaps you're wondering where this worm theology comes from anyway! King David in the Bible referred to himself as a worm. (Psalms 22:6). He called himself a worm not to make a statement about the worthlessness of human nature but to express his feelings. He was indicating that he felt like a worm that had been foresaken by God and scorned and despised by men.

Interestingly, this Psalm of David's is considered prophetic of Christ's experience on the cross. Jesus was quoting David in Psalm 22 when He said, "My God, why have you forsaken me?" When Jesus took on Himself the ugliness of our sin He was forsaken by God. At that painful moment of total rejection from men and God, He too felt like a worm. To say that the Bible tells us to think of ourselves as worms has no more basis than to say that the Bible tells us to think of Christ as a worm! God would not call us the apple of His eye (Deuteronomy 32:10) if we were merely worms to be stepped on by any passerby. Imagine Jesus presenting us to God, not as shiny red apples that have been redeemed and made holy, but as apples filled with worms!

Fighting Against Feeling Inadequate

From the dark and hidden corners of life are heard the faint cries of inadequacy. "I feel so worthless, like I can't do anything well," mumbled one woman as she looked at the ground. Another tearfully cried out, "I hate being me. I'm no good." Surprisingly, a young man bravely admitted to me what he tried to hide from everyone: "I just don't feel like I have anything significant to offer the world. I don't know what I'm going to do." Another man insisted, "I'm just a facade. I act like I've got my life all together, but inside I'm a mess. I'm really a failure. My dad was right, I will never amount to anything." A young girl looking for sympathy said, "I feel like a loser. I'll never do anything right. God must have been crazy to have made me."

You've heard these painful cries before. Psychologists say this emotional pain is evidence of "low self-esteem." If you don't suffer from it then you know someone who does. But even if you think you have a basically healthy self-esteem you probably have your moments—moments when that dreadful feeling of inadequacy tries to overtake you. Most people must battle these fears of inadequacy. Some of us raise the white flag and give in to feelings of inadequacy even before defeat is assured. Others charge forward with determination to prove that they are indeed adequate. Those who retreat from the threat of failure can easily be seen to lack a positive self-esteem. They don't see themselves as being good enough to conquer the obstacles and meet the challenges. On the other hand, those who charge forward toward success are usually thought to have good self-esteem. On the surface they feel good about themselves and they're confident that they are capable. It would seem that if the ones who give in to low self-esteem would learn to charge forward and fight like the others they'd have better self-esteem.

At one time Kristi and I both thought that was true. Early in our marriage it became clear that she gave in to low self-esteem while I fought to prove I wasn't as inadequate as I felt. She doubted herself and acted as if she was inadequate. For me it was the reverse. I was full of confidence on the outside and acted as if I was super-adequate. We discovered that underneath the contrasting impressions we gave to other people we both were fighting against feelings of inadequacy. The only difference was that Kristi had accepted and acted out her self-degrading feelings, whereas I was still trying to prove that I wasn't as inadequate as I felt deep inside.

People who share Kristi's experience are very aware of feeling bad about themselves. In Kristi's case, she knew she had a low self-esteem. She was guilty of the "M&M's"—maximizing her weaknesses and minimizing her strengths.[1] Sometimes she felt literally overcome by feelings of worthlessness, inadequacy, and self-hatred. She was quick to put herself down—even in front of other people. When people criticized her or took advantage of her she simply accepted it. This mistreatment only served to reinforce and reconfirm her low opinion of herself. Spiritually, she justified her negative self-esteem by calling it "humility." She thought God wanted her to think poorly of herself to bring glory to Him.

On the other hand, people who share my experience of being a seemingly confident achiever are not usually aware of having negative self-esteem. On the outside I appeared to be the model of high self-esteem. Some people even thought I was "cocky" at times. I believed things like, "I can do anything I set my mind to do!" or, "I don't need anyone else's help." I was like a maniac on a freeway, constantly swerving in and out of lanes to pass the people in front of me. I felt I had to get in front of everyone I ran into on the road of life in order to prove I was successful. My efforts to succeed were motivated by feelings that I wasn't good enough and would only feel good about myself if I was better than the person ahead of me. I justified my determination to succeed as advancing the kingdom of God. "After all," I 'd say, trying to cite Scripture in my defense, "the days are evil and I must make the most of every opportunity" (*see* Ephesians 5:15, 16).

Kristi and I realized that just as much as we were different in our surface attitudes toward ourselves we were similar in our underlying feelings. We both felt that we had to measure up to incredibly high standards in order to be acceptable. I wasn't the only one with idealistic self-expectations which I pressured myself to fulfill. Kristi also had high expectations for herself. And she wasn't alone in her feelings of inadequacy. I secretly felt inadequate and even used belittling self-condemnations to motivate myself to achieve. We both felt we weren't acceptable and lovable as we were and that we had to prove we were adequate by realizing our ideals for ourselves.

The Internal Critic

Whichever of the two of us you identify with most closely, you're probably aware of the internal critic driving you from within. It can be referred to as your "punitive self" or "condemning conscience." It has standards, ideals, and goals for you to measure up to and in this sense it creates your "ideal self." This punitive self is the voice of our inner parent. It develops in response to the judgments and evaluations of our parents and other people we look up to. It's no wonder "we sometimes scold ourselves with the exact words and tones of voice that our parents used."[2]

This internal ideal critic is born out of feelings of insecurity. We feel anxious about whether or not we'll be accepted as we are by our parents and others, so we try to become the ideal they want us to be. Many of us have tried to resolve this fear of not being good enough to be loved by developing incredibly high self-expectations. Even people who feel they can't measure up to other's expectations are still likely to hang on to their lofty standards. In fact, like the overconfident achievers, these self-doubters also tend to take great pride in their exalted standards—even calling them "godly." Their pride in their godlike ideals keeps them from letting go of them. It is the immense grandiosity of this ideal self that makes many people feel inadequate.

The combination of the grandiose ideals and critical judgments of our internal critic causes a split in the personality. It's as if one becomes two totally separate people—an impoverished and inadequate person hidden away inside and a grandiose and exalted person on the outside. Most of us try to show people our ideal self in order to gain their acceptance. Meanwhile, even if others applaud our facade and put us on a pedestal to be admired, inside we feel inadequate and insecure. *If other people really knew me they wouldn't like me,* we think. Our true self becomes scrunched under the weight of the pedestal on which our false ideal self proudly stands. We develop what might be called an "imposter complex," pretending to be someone we're not and fighting against the nagging fear that people will discover the person we really are inside.[3]

This internal critic is part of the internalized parent we talked about in chapter three. It's your internal parent that has idealistic self-expectations for you and is quick to criticize and condemn you for not being a "good enough Christian." It's the cruel perpetrator of the crime of murdering your self-esteem. It can also cause spiritual havoc in your life because it is the foundation upon which you build your God Image. When you internalize negative and punitive attitudes people have expressed toward you, it's natural to expect that others will treat you in the same way. In this case the sound of God's loving voice can easily get distorted through the loudspeaker of your internal critic.

The Dirt We Crawl In

Kristi and I have found that people who have wormlike self-images also have unloving God Images. Spiritually, it's as if they've been crawling around in the dirt of their negative images of God until they start to feel and act like worms! Psychological research seems to confirm this correlation between unloving God Images and low self-acceptance.[4] One study with a group of Christians found that those who viewed God as loving and kind had the highest levels of self-esteem, while those who perceived God to be vindictive, angry, impersonal, stern, and controlling had low levels of self-esteem.[5] A similar connection was made by the Apostle John who said, "We love because he first loved us" (1 John 4:19). To really love God and other people we need to first receive God's love. Usually, those who have trouble experiencing God's love have self-esteem problems going back to a childhood when they didn't feel valued by people important to them.

In fact, for all of us, the way we view ourselves ultimately goes back to the way we view God. Theologically God comes first as our Creator and our view of Him influences everything else in our lives including our self-esteem. Remember the figure

''How Perfect Love Becomes Painful'' from chapter 3? As this figure shows, our self-image problems relate to our God Image problems. We all need to receive God's love through people in order to develop a healthy self-esteem. This process breaks down when we perceive that the significant people in our lives don't completely love us as we are. When we don't feel totally acceptable to other people it's hard to really feel God's loving acceptance. The result is low self-esteem. (*See* appendix I to see each of the possible damaged areas in your self-image and the corresponding trouble spots in your God Image.)

This was true for one woman who experienced God as being critical and condemning. Her spiritual cry was like Rodney Dangerfield's famous line: ''I don't get no respect.'' She felt she wasn't worthy of God's acceptance. ''God expects so much of me,'' she moaned. ''I try my best to be a good Christian and it's still not good enough. He's so critical of me.'' Her spiritual life was ruled by the Critical Scrooge God. Her false god was like a movie critic who watched a film of her life, took detailed notes of its shortcomings, and then critically pointed out all her weaknesses.

Nick had a similar experience in his relationship with God. He described it this way: ''It's like I'm up on stage giving a piano recital in front of the great 'cloud of witnesses' and God is the chief witness—my old and crotchety piano teacher. I feel terrible because I can see that He's embarrassed by my performance.''

Others with self-esteem problems may have a slightly different image of God that is equally as unloving. Rick was a lanky teenager with an acne-splotched face, thick black glasses, and greasy hair that hung in his eyes. He obviously felt like one of the tragedies of adolescence and played the part of one of society's castaways. Even at church he didn't feel accepted. He got especially down on himself when he didn't make the church choir and the teacher told him it was because of his appearance. He was convinced that God was down on him also. He wanted so badly to be included and accepted. He had a false image of God as the Vain Pharisee God. It was as if God wouldn't accept Rick into

His choir of heavenly hosts. He wasn't good enough so God and all the heavenly singers just walked by him, thumbing their noses and looking the other way. Rick made the mistake of projecting onto God the rejecting attitudes of people in his church.

Another common negative God Image that contributes to feelings of low self-esteem is that of a "terrorist God" who is like a critical and demanding parent.[6] This mistaken view of a Terrorist God wears two different disguises—either that of the Outtagetcha Police Detective God in a trench coat and dark glasses or the Demanding Drill Sergeant God in a military uniform and holding a big stick.

A good friend of mine named Bob met this terrorist false god at a Christian Bible college in the South. A devout Christian, he recalled this time in his life as one in which he was the victim of "fundamentalist bashing." The type of Christianity he encountered there was extremely rigid, legalistic, and condemning. He felt emotionally thrashed and beaten up by some of the well-meaning Christian leaders at this school. The cruel, ungodly words of the dean of his school still ring in his ears: "If you're not careful you're going to miss God's will for your life and end up a knickknack on the back shelf of God's five-and-dime." Bob became motivated to serve God out of guilt and fear rather than love. In the process his self-esteem was bashed in the head by the beatings of a vicious and savage false god that carried a big stick.

From Worm to Butterfly

If you struggle with a wormlike self-image (whether it's obvious or hidden underneath an outer attitude of confidence), your question is: "How can I stop crawling in my dirty God Images?" The key is to emotionally redefine your image of God. You need to see God as having created you to be a butterfly and not a worm. Indeed, we all feel like worms at times and in a sense we are worms—worms being transformed into butterflies! There is a big difference between seeing yourself as a worm and seeing yourself as a beautiful butterfly in the making! God created mankind to be as butterflies but our sin has cast us into "spiritual wormhood." God solved the problem of our sin by sending His Son Jesus to be our Savior so that through Christ we can be transformed from worms to butterflies. As Christians we are to form our self-identity and self-esteem around this saving fact that we are butterflies in the making.

So many Christians identify themselves as worms or "wretched sinners." In doing this they are defining who they are around what the Apostle Paul calls the "old self" (Ephesians 4:22–24; Colossians 3:9, 10). The old self is the person one was before becoming a Christian. It's our identity apart from Christ. But Paul says we are now "in Christ," righteous before God, and in intimate relationship with Him through Christ (Ephesians 1). We have become "new creatures" (*see* 2 Corinthians 5:17). In Christ we are each now a "new self." This new self is a glorious child of God in the making. It's not a worm crawling on the ground, but a butterfly breaking out of its cocoon. We need to accept and esteem this new self as the fruit of God's Spirit within us. It's not the new self, but the old self that is a dirty and wretched worm that we are to hate and deny because it is contrary to God's redeeming and sanctifying work in us. To identify ourselves as worms is to deny that we are becoming butterflies through the work of God's Spirit in us.

Theologically, many Christians make one of two extreme errors—that of false humility or that of false pride. To be falsely humble is to crawl around like a worm, failing to see that you are a butterfly in the making. To be falsely proud is to fly high in the sky and forget that you once were a worm and were you to lose the breath of God's Spirit within you, you'd once again be a mere worm. Those who feel like worms often think that they must earn God's love because they are not acceptable as they are. Those who deny they ever were worms tend to feel that they have already earned God's love. Neither of these extremes is the answer to low self-esteem. An earthworm can't prove he's a butterfly, and a butterfly can't prove he was never a worm.

Instead, we need to accept that as Christians we are in the process of being transformed into beautiful butterflies. We can do this only when we emotionally grasp the grace our Loving Lord extends to us, even though we haven't earned it.

The image of God that we need to see is the picture of God that Jesus gave us in the parable of the prodigal son. Even though the prodigal rejected his father, disgraced his family name in wild living, and made a total failure of himself, the father lovingly received him back. The son felt like the pigs whose food he ate and the father gave him a robe of royalty. The son felt like a helpless failure who couldn't be trusted and the father gave him his signet ring of power and authority. The son felt like a mere slave and the father gave him shoes to put on his feet to symbolize his reacceptance into the family. The son felt he needed to work his way back into favor and the father threw a party for him to celebrate the new life he freely gave to his son. The father wouldn't let the son earn his way back into the family but accepted him as he was—clothes tattered, smelling of pigs and booze, and head hung low.

If deep inside you sometimes feel inadequate and that you must satisfy your "Heavenly Critic" to feel better about yourself, then picture the Loving Father. He opens His arms wide and runs out to embrace you, just as He did for His dirty, drunken son who did everything wrong. Only the unconditional love of our Heavenly Father can enable us to feel truly adequate. We can receive that love when we replace the condemning false god that rules our lives with an image of the Accepting God who loves and cares for us unconditionally. The Real God doesn't treat us like worms! He doesn't demand that we earn His love; He doesn't expect us to make up for our inadequacies. Instead, He replaces our weaknesses with His strength and makes us truly adequate. He freely gives us His love and seeks to transform us into glorious new creatures in Christ.

Questions for Reflection and Discussion

1. What do you think about ''worm theology''? Do you believe, feel, talk, or act as if you're a worm? Have you ever felt ''preached down to'' as though you were a dirty, slimy worm?

2. How does having a good, loving, and biblically accurate image of God help you as a Christian to realize your glorious inheritance and identity in Christ?

3. What is your ''internal critic'' (punitive self or condemning conscience) like? Do you ever feel helpless to meet the demands of your internal critic? Or do you like the challenge? How do you experience the voice of your internal critic compared to your experience of the voice of God?

4. What is your reaction to the illustration that as a Christian you're no longer a worm but are a butterfly, not an old self but a new self? Describe the difference between what you're like apart from Christ (old self) versus what you're like in Christ (new self). In what ways might you hate your old self and love your new self?

5. Would you be more likely to slip to the extreme of false humility (pretending to still be a dirty worm) or false pride (acting as if you don't need God's help to fly like a butterfly)? With your answer in mind what do you need to do to regain the right balance?

6. Prayerfully meditate on the parable of the prodigal son in Luke 15:11–32. Imagine yourself in the prodigal's shoes. You've just failed your Heavenly Father terribly and are walking home with your head hung low. Then picture God as your Loving Father that runs to you with arms open wide to hug and bless you! Your Father God loves you even though you don't deserve it and can't earn it. How does this picture of God's loving grace impact your self-esteem?

6
Can I Really Trust God?

But now you have broken down our walls, leaving us without protection.

Psalms 80:12 TLB

In Psalm 80 Asaph cries out to God on behalf of the Israelites, who had become the scorn of the surrounding nations, Asaph is convinced that God has angrily rejected His people forever. He poetically forms his feelings into a prayer to God, describing Israel as a tender vine that God brought from Egypt and planted. Asaph said that God cleared and tilled the land and nurtured Israel's growth until they were as a forest of mighty cedar trees that cast their shadows on the mountains.

"But then," Asaph moans to God, "you broke down our walls of divine protection so that the boars from the forest tore up our roots and the wild animals fed on our branches and leaves. Then our enemies came and chopped us down and burned us up.'' In desperation Asaph closes his prayer by saying, ''Revive us to trust in you, Lord.'' From Asaph's words we can see that the Israelites felt abused and trampled on. All their glory and success had been taken from them. Some of them blamed God for their misfortunes and were so angry at Him that they were rebelling against His authority. Asaph prayed for Israel's trust in God to be revived because they all were struggling to trust a God they felt had abandoned them.

Have you ever felt that God failed to protect you from some harm or left you in a vulnerable position? For some people, trusting God on a gut level is not easy. Intellectually they know God as the ''giver of good gifts,'' but emotionally it's as if He is a ''giver of bad gifts.'' God says to them, ''Ask from me and I will give you what you ask. Knock, and I'll open the door to your dreams.'' But they are afraid to knock on heaven's door for fear of getting a stone when they asked for bread or getting a snake when they asked for a fish. Clearly, this negative picture of God is the exact opposite of the Loving Father God that Jesus was talking about in Matthew 7:7–12. And many times people who struggle to emotionally trust God know this.

Kristi and I each became aware of this problem by accident. We knew that deep down people needed and wanted to have a special relationship with God as their Daddy, or ''Abba'' as He is referred to in Scripture. Like the Apostle Paul said, the spirits of all true children of God cry out, ''Abba, Father'' (Galatians 4:6). After all, we all have a delicate little child within us, don't we? This inner child needs to be held and sensitively loved. Individually, Kristi and I tried to apply this truth in our counseling. We learned the hard way that some Christians don't want God to be their Daddy!

In my case, I prayed for a woman I was counseling that Abba would hold her in His lap, stroke her hair, look into her eyes, and say He loved her. When we were through praying I was surprised to see she was crying and looked disturbed. Then she told me that her adopted father had molested her when she was a little girl.

Naturally, I felt awful. I had just caused God to abuse her! Not really, but it felt like it to her.

Kristi had a similar experience with a middle-aged woman she counsels. Kristi was having this woman meditate on some positive images of God as a Loving Father as a form of healing prayer. In a matter of seconds, the client regressed emotionally and started talking like a little girl afraid of being sexually abused by her father. Fortunately, Kristi wisely switched to an image of God as "our Friend, Jesus" which enabled this woman to reground herself in reality.

Neither of these women could trust God as Father. They were carrying terribly painful memories of being abused by their earthly fathers. They needed to relate to safe images of God as a trusted Friend or a caring Shepherd. Before you dismiss these experiences as "happening to only a few unfortunate women who have been abused," you need to realize that somewhere between 25 percent and 35 percent of women have been sexually abused. And as many as 15 percent of men have been abused sexually, usually by another male. Also, it's not only people who have been abused who have trouble trusting God. Difficulty trusting God affects sweeping numbers of Christians who have felt betrayed by someone they trusted, unfairly treated by an authority figure, preached at and condemned by religious figures, or just plain let down time and again by people on whom they relied.

It's so important that all of us who are people helpers—whether professional psychotherapists, pastors, educators, or lay counselors—be aware of this delicate issue.

> When we ask individuals to trust God and to surrender to Him, we are presuming they have concepts/feelings of a trustworthy God who has only their best interests at heart and in whose hands they can place their lives. But according to their deepest gut-level concept of God, they may hear us asking them to surrender to an unpredictable and fearful ogre, an all-powerful monster whose aim is to make them miserable and take from them the freedom to enjoy life.[1]

Surely I Can Trust God!

On a conscious level most of us think we can trust God. He is God! If we can't trust our Creator and the Great Lover of the world then whom can we trust? Despite the insistence of our conscious minds, at a deeper level we may fear relying totally on God. Our subconscious pictures of God may be blended with our pictures of other significant people in our lives to whom we've related. Often we don't realize this. We assume that things are fine spiritually because we believe and do all the right things. Yet, emotionally we may be having some problems that are affecting us spiritually and we're not aware of it. Some Christians don't pay much attention to their emotions. Emotions are just the caboose, right? The train will run along fine without them! This is a grave mistake. If you want to have a fulfilling relationship with God and serve Him effectively then you must attend to your emotions. You especially must acknowledge the occasional inner hesitations that subtly and unconsciously may keep you from wholeheartedly entrusting yourself into your Heavenly Father's care.

Some people, instead of listening to their inner reservations and feelings of mistrust, try to force themselves to trust God. They say things like, "I should trust God." "I should give Him my all." "I should surrender all areas of my life to Him."

And so it goes, we "should" ourselves into trusting God and all the while we are unaware of how we really feel inside about trusting Him with the sensitive parts of ourselves. For some people this becomes a vicious cycle. The more they intellectually force themselves to trust God, the more they emotionally build a huge barrier between God and themselves. As this continues, it leads them to become emotionally estranged from the One they call Lord. From outward appearance it may look like these people have surrendered their whole lives to Christ. In reality, even though they are trying to be dedicated Christians, their unacknowledged inner fears and hesitations are keeping them from trusting God. Their spiritual ship has a leak and it's slowly sinking under the weight of denied feelings, which take the shape of various untrustworthy God Images.

I've Been Betrayed!

I saw Juan when he was an adolescent and lived with his mother and two younger brothers. His father had left the family when Juan was five. Juan was a "mama's boy" if there ever was one. He adored everything about his mom except that she was, in his words, a "holy nag." She was very religious and loving and wanted the best for her boy, so she often nagged and pushed and pried to make sure he was taken care of right.

In counseling, Juan and I were particularly focusing on his feelings about growing up without a father. To help him get in touch with and sort through his feelings, I had him record them in his own private journal. During the course of counseling, this journal took on increased significance as some of his feelings were quite painful and troublesome. Nearly every day Juan locked himself in his room and wrote in his journal. He learned to form his feelings into prayers to God as the Psalmists did. His mother began to be resentful though, feeling that Juan was closing her out of his life. One day when she was cleaning up his room she picked up his journal which he had left on his nightstand and started reading it! When Juan found out he felt deeply hurt and betrayed. "She says she loves me," he cried, "but why would she sneak around behind my back and pry into my private life? From now on I'm going to be more careful. I'll never be that trusting again."

When the person you trust most violates your trust—even if it seems innocent to the trespasser, as it did to Juan's mom—you tend to close up emotionally to other people as Juan did. If you've ever experienced this type of violation of your trust then you know what it's like to feel compelled to erect barriers and defenses against being hurt again. God has created us so that when we've been betrayed we have a natural instinct to protect ourselves from being taken advantage of again. This is what happened to Juan. He stopped recording his feelings for fear that they'd be trampled on again. He hid his emotions and vulnerabilities from everyone—even God. God became another "holy nag" like his mother. God acted nice and loving, but was really an undercover spy, trying to pry into Juan's private life. For a while, Juan was afraid to trust God because his image of Him was of the Indian Giver false god who promised love and blessing but suddenly pulled out the rug from under his feet.

Geoff also had difficulty fully trusting God. Like Juan, Geoff had a subconscious fear of being betrayed by God. Unlike Juan though, Geoff could not point to any one particular incident in which his trust was violated. In Geoff's case, he was trying so hard to trust God with his decision to go to seminary but was still feeling unsure. Then he had a dream that uncovered his problem. He dreamed he was walking up to the angel of the Lord for a blessing. He reverently kneeled before the angel who looked like a kind and wise old man. To Geoff's surprise though, the angel of the Lord began to put him down and humiliate him.

Then, in Geoff's words, "I got the left hand!" Like Esau in the Bible, Geoff missed the blessing of God that he sought. Instead of receiving the angel's right hand (a sign of blessing), he got the angel's left hand (a sign of cursing). Geoff was deeply distressed. When he looked up he saw that the angel now looked like an ugly and threatening monster! After Geoff talked to me about his troubling dream he realized that the reason he was having difficulty trusting God with his seminary decision was that he secretly feared God would not bless him. Geoff had a subconscious image of a mean God who might betray him.

Don't Push God on Me!

Liz also had trouble trusting God. Her image of God was of a Pushy Salesman God who would stick His foot in her door and force her to do things His way. In fact, when Liz came to me for counseling the first thing she said to me was, "You're not going to push God on me, are you?" Liz was very sensitive to being controlled, manipulated, or pushed around in any way. Ever since she was molested by her father, beginning when she was five years of age and continuing into her teens, Liz has been afraid of being taken advantage of by men. Liz had trouble trusting male authority figures in particular. Unfortunately, her fears extended to her Heavenly Father also.

Actually, the problem that brought Liz in for counseling was a marriage problem. She was resisting her husband's sexual advances because she said she couldn't trust him. In the four years they'd been married she'd had sex with him only if she initiated it. She told me that she felt guilty for not submitting to her husband, but she was too afraid to trust him. When she went to her pastor for counseling he said that she should start to "act" like she loved her husband and "force" herself to trust him and then the feelings would come. But her acting clearly wasn't working well.

Liz took her acting job into her relationship with God as well. The script to her "spiritual act" dictated that she should force herself to trust God even if it caused her to feel manipulated and taken advantage of. God was her Master, and she was to slavishly serve Him lest she be whipped into submission. It was an impossible script for her to trust the abusive and intimidating God she saw in her heart.

Her analogy was, "It's like God is the Potter and I'm His cheap lump of clay. He beats, pulls, and twists me into a mushy piece of clay that He can mold into whatever He wants, which has nothing to do with what I want to be." She had negatively caricatured God as a punitive and abusive potter who used her for His own selfish purposes. For Liz, emotionally trusting God was like trusting her abusive father when she was a little girl.

Instead of seeking God's healing comfort, Liz found herself trying to hide from God her terrible secret that she was abused and was now "spoiled" and "bad." Fortunately, because she wanted to trust God and other male figures, we had a place to start. First, we had to work through her feelings of having been abused and her fear of trusting men. Then I could help her relate to God as a gentle and caring Father who wouldn't force Himself on her. She could trust a God like this.

Regretfully, as I mentioned earlier, sexual abuse is far too common to treat lightly. To make matters worse, experts say that the statistics on the prevalence of sexual abuse show that it is just as common in religious homes as in nonreligious homes. And almost always, when it occurs a distorted image of God is the result. In fact, one study of people's images of God found that people who had been sexually abused had a significantly less loving image of God than did those who had not been sexually abused.[2] We need to listen to the cries of these hurting people:

> A 57-year-old woman cried: "When I hear you say that God loves me, I have a hard time trying not to remember Daddy raping me and saying, 'I love you—I love you—I love you,' all the time he was doing it to me. . . . Even after all these years, every time I hear the word God, I see Daddy's face."[3]
>
> A young woman explained: "My father always warned my sisters and I that if we ever did anything 'bad' or 'wrong' he would hang us by our hair and cut off our heads. Now my fear of my father is interfering with my relationship with God. The adult in me knows the difference. But there is a child back in there somewhere who can't seem to tell the difference between my daddy and God. Ever since, my sisters and I each have lived in fear of my daddy and have been scared to death of God."[4]
>
> A 19-year-old young man demanded: "Where was God when this was going on? If God is so big then why couldn't he stop it? I'll never trust anyone again, including God!"
>
> One woman expressed her feelings in a journal entry. "Dear Dad, I remember you covering my mouth to stifle my screams and the whole time telling me next time it won't hurt so much. I prayed . . . God please don't let him do this to me again. But God didn't hear my prayers and I prayed for his mercy every day for seven years."

This kind of emotional trauma invariably creates difficulty for people to trust God. I've found that people who grew up in alcoholic homes also tend to have trouble fully trusting God on an emotional level. Their image of God is often of a pushy and angry "Cosmic Alcoholic Parent" that is harsh, judgmental, and unforgiving.[5] This was the case for one man who said, "Every time I thought of trusting God as father, all I could see was my own drunken dad slamming me against the wall." This man and others like him need to emotionally disentangle God from their alcoholic fathers in order to really trust God as their gentle and loving Heavenly Father. This is not as easy as it sounds because the distorted God Images of those who have lived in an alcoholic home are connected with deep emotional wounds and long-standing dysfunctional patterns of behavior. Just like those who have been sexually abused, those who have been "co-dependent" with an alcoholic parent or spouse must engage themselves in a recovery process that involves reestablishing trust in God and others who can help them.

I'm Doing Things My Way

"I trusted God with everything and He blew it," exclaimed my good friend Matt. Matt had just been through a flood of tragedy in which he had been overcome by wave after wave of problems ending in the collapse of his business and his dreams of success. He was convinced it was all part of a secret divine plot against him. The God he had previously trusted with his life was now a Cosmic Con Artist. Matt imagined God to be like the slick, smooth-talking television preacher who asks for your money and then uses your sacrifice to go out and buy an elegant home in Palm Springs.

"God made me all these promises," said Matt, "so I went out on a limb and trusted Him only to find out that the limb couldn't hold my weight! God tricked me into trusting Him and then watched me fall to the ground! God is no longer trustworthy. His image as Omnipotent and All-Sovereign God is tarnished. The whole thing is a big scam!" For the moment, my friend found himself dodging God. He lost trust in God's authority and so he was spiritually "on the run," avoiding the demands and dictates of an unfair and manipulative Divine Dictator so that he could regain control of his life.

Many people like Matt have trouble with God being the authority. They feel He rules over them unjustly. Consequently, they rebel against God by shaking their fist at Him and saying, "From now on I'll run my life without You!" For some of these people, authority problems begin early in life. Their parents' manner of discipline is nonexistent, inconsistent, or overly strict. Or they learned as children that to get attention from people they had to be "bad." Or maybe they were just rebellious teenagers who didn't respect rules and wanted their own way. In any case, when people have problems submitting to and respecting authority, it shows up in their relationship with God. Their mistrust in God is usually rooted in distorted perceptions of God as an unjust Divine Dictator or a Cosmic Con Artist. In either case, the key to restoring trust in God is working through unresolved issues with past authority figures and discovering a clear image of the Trustworthy God who has our best interests at heart.

Doubting God

Some people's issues of mistrust in God are expressed in struggles of doubt or unbelief. Recently a friend of mine who was completing his college degree in theology went through a crisis of doubt. His doubts emerged when he found himself faced with apparent theological contradictions and a spiritual life that had become sterile and academic. He said his doubts came down to one question: "If God exists, then why doesn't He reveal Himself to me?" His image of God was of a Statue God—impersonal, distant, and existing on a philosophical rather than a practical level.

A young girl in high school had her doubts about God too. "How can I believe in a God who let my father die in a plane crash?" she asked me. Prior to her father's tragic death she had a strong faith in God. Now she was in inner turmoil and had abandoned her faith at a time when she needed it most. Her image of God was a Marshmallow God who didn't protect her father and so couldn't be trusted again.

A career woman was also doubting God. She had prayed that God would lead her to the right job and then found that she was unhappy at the job she felt He led her to. "God misled me!" she cried out. "Or maybe He was never there to lead me in the first place," she continued. Her doubts in God left her in a faith crisis. She lost trust in God when she felt that He hadn't guided her. Now she was questioning whether God even existed.

The doubts experienced by each of these three people can be traced back to a mistaken image of an untrustworthy God. It's sad when "a believer gets into his head such a wrong idea of God that it comes between him and God or between him and his trusting God. Since he does not recognize what he is doing he blames God rather than his faulty picture."[6]

It is difficult to trust God when you have a negative image of Him hidden in your subconscious. It's like a blind person trying to find his way in an unfamiliar area without his guide dog. He is sure to trip up along the way. When you're dealing with doubts about God's goodness and trustworthiness you need someone to guide you through your doubts. That's because doubt is a blinding emotion that contradicts faith. To continue in doubt is to be double-minded and unstable (James 1:6–8).

As hard as it is to face your feelings of doubt and mistrust for God it's the only way out. Just as you can't force yourself to trust God so you can't pretend you trust Him when you're emotionally hesitant and doubtful inside. Working through feelings of doubt and mistrust in God requires the willingness to risk and take a step of faith. It's like walking into a pitch black tunnel and not knowing if you'll see an onrushing train, the deadness of unending blackness, or a light at the end of the tunnel.

A Safe Refuge

Is there a light at the end of your tunnel of mistrust? If you've felt disappointed by God can you ever fully trust Him again?

Recovering from violations of your trust is not easy—no matter who has let you down. When it's God whom you feel has let you down, it's especially difficult to reestablish wholehearted trust in Him as an emotionally safe refuge. Oh, it's easy to say that you "trust God with everything." It's even easy to *think* that you're living as if you trust God. But, our trust level is really measured in terms of our emotions. The emotions of our hearts are at the very cores of our beings and must not be ignored in spiritual matters. Deep-seated feelings of mistrust and hesitation are among the most deadly of spiritual problems that we need to be careful not to "doctrinalize" away. The way to get over such feelings is to prayerfully go right through them. Express your feelings to God (even if they are negative feelings or issues of mistrust toward God) by writing or praying your own personal psalms.

This is what our Lord Jesus did on the eve before His crucifixion in the garden of Gethsemane. The gospel accounts make it quite clear that Jesus was literally overwhelmed with anguish and sorrow. He was struggling to submit His human will to His divine will. His humanity told Him that the cup of suffering ahead at Calvary was too much. His divinity told Him that to drink of this cup was to fulfill His purpose as the Christ. Jesus chose to trust the Father God (Mark 14:32–36). We need to remember that Jesus came to this choice by acknowledging and sharing His fearful and sorrowful human feelings of mistrust to God.

Some of us who have been blessed with loving relationships with family, friends, and mentors or disciplers have the maturity and strength to go straight to God with our feelings and don't need anyone else's help. For many of us though, this is not the case. At one time or another, we must seek the help of someone we respect in order to work through painful feelings of fear and inhibition that keep us from fully trusting God and others. I've found that if people are willing to take the risk and make the commitment to trust one person with their hidden feelings they can usually transfer this trust to God and to other people. If you do this, your trusted friend can become the bridge between your emotional pain and God, taking you from an untrustworthy God Image to a new image of a God you can trust with your life.

This was the case with Ken, one of the least likely types of persons to seek professional counseling. He was socially isolated and didn't seem to have a feeling bone in his body. He explained that his problem was difficulty trusting people enough to be vulnerable with them and open up emotionally. I discovered that this had been a pattern for Ken ever since he was a little boy and was smothered by his mother. In his relationship with his mother, and now with everyone, Ken saw two choices: allow himself to be suffocated by the other or withdraw completely and survive life alone.

Realizing what Ken needed, I asked him if he'd ever related to God as being like a nurturing mother hen as He is described in Psalm 91. To Ken, just the thought of such a relationship with God was like having a bucket of cold water dumped on his head! His relationship with God was very formal and impersonal; nothing like a caring and intimately loving relationship between a little chick and the mother hen!

Persisting with my initial assessment, I asked Ken to start meditating on Psalm 91, picturing himself as a chick cuddling up to his Heavenly Mother Hen in a nest. As you might imagine, this quickly brought to the surface his fears of being suffocated in relationships. Fortunately, Ken risked trusting me and sharing these feelings with me. I humbly became like a narrow, rickety old bridge that Ken dared to walk across. In the process, he went from slipping down the eroding cliff of an impersonal and untrustworthy image of God to standing atop the safe and secure cliff of a trusted image of a deeply personal and even nurturing God.

Our Abba desires to be a safe and secure refuge in the storms of life for all of us. The psalms of your heart are dear to your Heavenly Father and He wants nothing more than to record your personal psalms on the pages of His heart. He is ready to walk with you across the rickety old bridge of human relationships so that you can recover the intimacy and love that give birth to trust. If you're not ready for your Father God to hold your hand and walk with you, then He'll wait for you on the other side of the bridge. In the meantime, you might think of God as a Mother Hen, a Caring Shepherd, or your trusted Friend Jesus. You may even need to start where Asaph did. If you remember from the beginning of the chapter, he prayed, "Revive us to trust in you, Lord." In this case, make your prayer, "Lord, I trust You with my inability to trust. I want to trust You, help my mistrust."

Questions for Reflection and Discussion

1. What's your reaction to the idea that God is like a mother? a nurturing mother hen that feeds and protects her little chick in a safe nest (Psalm 91)? a mother eagle that topples her little eagle from the nest when it's time to teach it to fly (Deuteronomy 32:9–15)? a mother nursing her baby (Isaiah 49:13–15)? What do each of these pictures do for your level of emotional trust in God?

2. It's in times of extreme difficulty or suffering that it's hardest to trust God. Read Jeremiah 15:18 and then think of a time of personal suffering and the feelings you had toward God at that time. It was during a time of emotional pain that Jeremiah likened trusting God to trying to cross an untrustworthy and deceptive river. When was the last time that you stepped out to trust God only to find yourself carried downstream by a vicious current of hardship that thrashed you against the rocks?

3. Do you believe God has a special and unique plan for your life? Do you believe that He helps you discover and carry out that plan? Meditate on Psalm 23. Picture God as your Shepherd and yourself as one of His sheep and then follow the Psalm 23 scene from the grassy meadows to the quiet waters to the path of righteousness. . . into the valley of the shadow of death and finally into the house of the Lord. What's the hardest part of the meditation for you: leaving the restful meadow by the peaceful waters? finding the "right" path? trusting that God is with you in the valley? persevering through the valley? trusting that God has shown you the way in your heart and you can complete the path knowing that He is following right behind you? going into the house of

the Lord and thanking God for His goodness to you during your suffering in the valley? Consider the issues of trust at each step in your journey with your Shepherd.

4. What is your style of trusting God? Do you blindly and optimistically step out into things and "hope for the best"? Or do you make decisions very carefully and cautiously? Do you decide for yourself what is best and then ask for God's blessing? Or do you expect Him to show you what is best before you've decided what you want?

5. Picture God as your Potter and yourself as the clay He molds and shapes into a vessel (Jeremiah 18:1–6; Isaiah 45:9–11; 64:8). Are you soft or hard clay? Can you trust your Potter to gently mold and shape you? If you let Him mold you, will you like the vessel He makes you into? What kind of vessel does He make you into? Do you have any say in what He makes you into or does God have all the say?

6. In the New Testament Jesus is called "Lord." Paul even uses the analogy that He is our Master and we are His slaves (Romans 6:16–23). Can you picture yourself as God's slave? Can you trust Him to treat you as a friend or as a son or daughter even though you're only a slave? If you resist the idea of "bonding" yourself as a slave to your Master then explore your feelings and try to understand why it's hard for you to trust God this way. If you're not Jesus' slave then whose slave are you? parents? spouse? money? work? achievement? pleasure? drugs? emotional pain? sin?

7

I Have to Be Perfect

(And Then God Will Be Pleased With Me)

Be perfect, therefore, as your heavenly Father is perfect.

Matthew 5:48

To many people, Jesus seems to be saying in the quote above that we should strive to be perfect. One survey that included mostly Christians indicated that 84 percent of the people polled admitted to having perfectionistic tendencies.[1] No matter what the actual percentage of Christians who are perfectionists is, many of us would admit that we ourselves are perfectionists in certain areas of our lives, or at least that we know other people who are. We tend to justify our perfectionistic strivings on spiritual grounds, reasoning that since God is perfect we also have to be perfect if we want to please Him. But do Jesus' words "Be perfect as God is perfect" really mean that God is a "Holy Perfectionist" and we must strive to be perfect and faultless?

Indeed "God is truly Perfection, but He is no Perfectionist."[2] God knows better than anyone else that we are actually quite imperfect and could never be perfectly devoted to Him even if He demanded it from us. Instead, He makes us aware of the great gap between His perfection and our imperfection and then, in the gift of salvation through faith in Christ, He gives us His perfection so that we can stand before Him as if we were as perfect as He is. This gift of grace which theologians call "justification" actually enables us to become more and more perfect, not by our striving for perfection but by receiving His grace and power. The Pharisees in Jesus' day missed this divine grace and tried to attain perfection by their own efforts. Jesus severely condemned them for their prideful and ungodly perfectionism.

Even though, "there is a great difference between true Christian perfection and perfectionism,"[3] Kristi and I have found that many Christians confuse the two. Instead of resting in the finished work of Christ at the cross that freely bestows upon them God's perfection, they struggle as the Pharisees did to attain divine perfection by living up to grandiose standards and expectations. They become performance-focused Christians, trying to earn the free grace of God.

One December, just before the beginning of the new year, a perfectionist said to me, "This year I'm going to live up to my commitments and please God." Around the same time of year another perfectionist had the opposite reaction. Giving up hope of ever doing enough to please God, she said, "This year I'm not going to even try to be good enough for God. I just can't do everything that He wants me to do. I never live up to those New Year's resolutions I make to God anyway." Even though these two people reacted differently to the standards they thought God had for them, they suffered from the same problem: Neither of them experienced God's love and acceptance because they felt they had to be perfect to earn it, when actually it was a free gift they could only receive by faith.

Perfectionists tend to live by a secret lie that says, "If only I can be perfect (or at least better than I am), God will be pleased with me.'' This inner belief that drives them is doubly destructive because they are never able to reach the perfection they strive for and also because no matter how well they do things, they cannot earn God's love and acceptance. Thus they are doomed from the start to feel inadequate at their failure to do the impossible and to feel rejected by God's apparent lack of love for them. Such perfectionists are projecting onto God their own demands for perfection and their own conditional self-acceptance. The feelings of inadequacy or rejection that they struggle to avoid are due to their distorted image of God as a perfectionist who loves them only if they meet His standards.

David Stoop, in his book *Living With a Perfectionist,* notes that perfectionism almost invariably leads to distorted God Images. He says that the perfectionists he works with have a fear-inducing image of God as a ''spiritual terrorist'' who is really more like a demanding and critical parent.[4] This spiritual terrorist whom perfectionists call ''God'' insists on perfection at all costs. He dresses himself as either the Demanding Drill Sergeant God who pushes people to be more and more perfect or as the Outtagetcha Police Detective God constantly checking up on people and pointing out their every mistake.

These gods of ''absolute perfection''[5] are false gods that cause perfectionists to live their spiritual lives with one foot on the gas and the other foot on the brake. These perfectionists drive themselves crazy by revving up their spiritual engines to push themselves to measure up to incredibly high demands while at the same time slamming on their spiritual brakes to carefully hold themselves back from making mistakes that would displease God.

I Should Be a Better Christian

Have you ever told yourself that you should be a better Christian? So many of us have, and how could we not when we hear sermon after sermon that seems to say, ''You're not living as you should! You better get your spiritual act together or you'll be in trouble with God!" It's as if God is glaring down with a frown on His face, shaking His finger at us while He reruns a tape called the "Christian should list." It goes like this: "You should pray more. You don't witness as much as you should. You ought to be more involved in church. You should be more self-disciplined. You shouldn't indulge in such sinful thoughts. You should work harder. You should do this. You shouldn't do that. . . ."

The list goes on and on and we feel more and more guilty and inadequate because we can't begin to live up to all these shoulds. Those who carry a list of spiritual shoulds in their heads probably feel crushed at times under the weight of their image of an impossibly demanding and unpleasable God.

David Seamands who is a pastor in Kentucky and is on the staff of Asbury Theological Seminary has done extensive work with Christians who struggle with perfectionism. He describes the struggle of the many perfectionists who always feel that they "should have," "could have," or "would have" done better.

> Try as you will, you always remain in second, not first place. And since you and God always demand first place, that's not quite good enough. So, back to the spiritual salt mines you go, with increased efforts to please yourself and an increasingly demanding God who is never quite satisfied. But you always fall short, you are inadequate, you never arrive but you must never stop trying.[6]

Perfectionists can't stop trying to "do all they should" and can never feel "good enough" until they emotionally redefine their image of God. "They are running as fast as they can on the treadmill of their perfectionism, and God is the One who keeps turning up the speed. He's the One demanding they run faster,"[7]

One woman kept trying harder and harder to please God but still felt inadequate. Her distorted God Image came out in a dream in which she pictured God as a magician in black evening dress. He was doing magic tricks and constantly bowing to applause from spectators. He had a dog, cat, and rabbit that were trained to jump through a hoop when He called their names, which were Moses, Isaac, and Joseph. In her dream, this woman felt like she was fourth in line. God would call her name and she'd have to jump through a hoop for Him. As a child she could never say her prayers properly enough for her father, so in her dream she couldn't jump through God's hoops right![8]

Do you ever feel as if you can't keep up the pace on God's treadmill or you have to jump through one hoop after another for God? If so you may be trying to please the Demanding Drill Sergeant God. People who labor under the burden of a demanding God often feel secretly angry at God or that they want to avoid Him. Often their uncomfortable feelings are pushed back down inside of themselves for fear that they might be sinful or displeasing to God. Meanwhile, the perfectionist's resentment builds until he finally realizes that "his resentment is against a caricature of a god who is never satisfied. A god whom he can never please no matter how hard he tries, no matter what he gives up or holds on to."[9] Perfectionists become enslaved by this Demanding Drill Sergeant who keeps upping the ante and demanding a little bit more from them. The only way they can gain freedom from their religious perfectionism is to acknowledge their feelings and discover God's free grace.

God Will Getcha!

Some of us feel that we have to carefully tiptoe our way through life in hopes that God won't jump out of the bushes and yell, "Gotcha!" We're afraid of getting caught doing something wrong that we didn't even know was wrong. So we become fearful of making any mistakes at all. With our overly cautious attitude, we find we're always looking over our shoulders in order to avoid the "Heavenly Snoop" called the Outtagetcha Police Detective God.

To protect ourselves from this "Gotcha God" in the detective's trench coat and dark glasses we may become legalistic and overly scrupulous. We say to ourselves, "If only I can perfectly follow all of God's commands, I'll be okay.'' Then if we feel that we are successful in avoiding all appearances of evil, we can hide behind our self-made halos and feel safe from the judgment and criticism of our Legalistic God.

One perfectionist I counsel has a distorted God Image of a Gotcha God. He often hesitates to do what he really wants, saying, ''But I'm not sure what God thinks about that.'' He is so concerned about whether or not he is measuring up to God's standards and if he'd come out ahead on God's balance sheet that he gets paralyzed with fear. In his ''spiritual paranoia'' he fears that God will be upset with him if he doesn't do just the right thing in just the right way at just the right time. So in order to feel good about doing even the smallest things, he feels he must always check to see if God will give him a nod of approval. He's trying so hard to earn God's approval that he can't just relax and be the person God created him to be.

The inner insecurity of anxious perfectionists like this man makes them easy prey to the evaluations and criticisms of other people, especially of other Christians they respect. With every sermon such people introspect and say to themselves,

> Ah-h, maybe that's what's wrong with me. Maybe if I give this up . . . add that to my life . . . . Maybe if I stop doing this or I start doing that, I will experience peace, joy, and power. Maybe then God will accept me, and I will please Him.[10]

People with this type of legalistic perfectionism are focusing their lives on external rules and standards rather than internal principles. They are ruled by fear rather than love and avoiding the bad rather than pursuing the good. They usually feel anxious and have overly sensitive consciences. It is from their guilt-ridden consciences that these people draw their images of God.

When I gave one anxious and scrupulous woman a pencil and piece of paper and asked her to draw a picture of what she felt God was like, she drew a pair of sinister eyes on a billboard as was portrayed in the novel *The Great Gatsby*. I asked a second perfectionist to tell me what his image of God was like and he said: "To me it is as if God is a Divine Patrolman in an unmarked police car and He has set a speed trap for me and is waiting for me to come flying down the hill so He can pull me over and ticket me." For these people, the distorted image of a Gotcha God creates so much anxiety that they live life looking over their shoulders to see if God is watching them with sinister eyes.

Being the Ideal Christian

People who push themselves to achieve unrealistically high standards or carefully try to avoid any wrongdoing or mistakes often fall into a deceptive and deadly trap. They are likely to repress their "real self," which they feel isn't good enough, and try and be their "ideal self," which seems to be admired and accepted by people they look up to. The reality of their feelings of inadequacy are minimized and they identify themselves with the idealistic image of what they feel they should be. They pretend to be someone they're not. Psychologist Karen Horney referred to this process as "the search for glory" because it represents a striving to be a perfectionistic ideal that one is not.[11] Spiritually, this is manifested in the person who says to himself, "Since other people can't accept me as I am, I must not be good enough for God either. I can only be accepted and approved of if I can be this ideal person who I should be."

A friend of mine named Sam told me that he has always pressured himself to be the "ideal Christian" he felt he should be. Sam grew up in a strict religious home that was largely devoid of emotional closeness and affection. As a boy he felt that the only way he got recognition in his family was if he was active in the church, read his Bible every day, had good things to say during family devotions before dinner, and did the other spiritual things that his parents wanted him to do. Sam learned to "act the part" of a model Christian because it got him attention, but when he was away from his parents he wasn't such a perfect Christian.

The unspoken messages in Sam's home were: "We will love you if . . . ." "We will approve of you when . . . ." "You will be accepted by us because . . . ." It was natural for Sam to transfer these messages from his parents to God. As an adult, the only way Sam could feel close to God and feel good about himself as a Christian was if he measured up to the conditions and ideals he thought God had for him. Sam felt he had to be this ideal Christian, but in his real self he felt inadequate.

David Seamands refers to this struggle that many Christians like Sam have as the conflict between "Super You" and "Real You." He says that Super You is an ideal self that is a false and idealistic image of what you think you must be in order to be loved and accepted. He sometimes asks people to think about whether they bring their ideal or real self to God when they pray or meditate and they often respond saying something like:

> It's hard to imagine that God could accept the real me that is so sinful and inadequate. I fall so far short of the person I'm supposed to be. I want so badly to be that ideal me and someday I will be. So I don't want God to pay attention to this inadequate me that is temporary. When I'm a more perfect Christian and do all that I should for God, I know God will accept me.
>
> I guess I try to put my best spiritual foot forward and make sure I have my finest halo on. I want God to see the ideal me and then I'll know He accepts me.[12]

Have you ever pretended to be the perfect person or the ideal Christian? Many of us have. The tragedy of being "Super You" is that other people don't see the real you inside. Underneath your Super You mask you're left wondering, *If others really knew me would they accept me?* Out of fear the real you has been hidden way inside yourself. When we hide that real self from others it usually gets hidden from God, too, so that we don't even feel His unconditional love and acceptance. In such cases we subconsciously imagine God will be like the people for whom we felt we couldn't be good enough. Our image of Him becomes distorted to seem like a God of Absolute Perfection who accepts only an ideal self. So to feel accepted by God and others, we stand proudly atop the tallest pedestal that we can find, not realizing that our acceptance is a false one because our real self is being squashed underneath the pedestal of perfectionism we've built.

Perfect Grace

The only healing for perfectionism is through seeing a true image of the Real God and experiencing His perfect grace. The grace of God is His free, undeserved, and unearnable love and favor that He extends to the real you (Ephesians 2:8–10). You may love your ideal self because people admire that self, and this helps motivate you to succeed. But God hates this false idealized image because it is prideful and it keeps you from receiving the gracious love He extends to your real self. The perfectionistic ideal we think we should be must die, for it is part of the old self that has been crucified with Christ (Romans 6:6). We must dare to show God the insecurities and deficiencies of our real selves so that we can begin to receive His loving grace and unconditional acceptance that will heal our insecurities and strengthen our weaknesses. Opening up our real selves to God is a process that takes time. We must pour our hearts out to Him in prayer, expressing our feelings and meditating upon the truth of God's grace in Scripture (*see* chapters 9 and 10).

This process of receiving the grace of the Loving God is not easy for perfectionists. They can read in the Bible promises and illustrations of God's love that reveal Him to be a good and gracious God and still want to hide the weaknesses of their real selves from Him. "The tendency of perfectionists is to read those verses and say, 'Yes, but. . . .' And after the 'but' comes the list of things that they must do to 'deserve' whatever God wants to give them."[13]

Perfectionists like this have been negatively programmed so that a tape runs and reruns in their subconscious minds telling them that they must measure up to unrealistic standards, can't make a mistake or have problems, and have to show that they are some super ideal. They feel they must do these things in order to be accepted by others. Rewriting these tapes of conditional acceptance is usually a process that involves working through the hurt and anger experienced in relationships with others. God usually becomes one of the others.

The Apostle Paul sought to help the Christians at Colossae grow out of religious perfectionism. Perhaps the church at Colossae was full of perfectionists even as many of our churches are today! Paul showed the Colossian perfectionists that the way to please God wasn't by living up to spiritual shoulds, legalistic standards, and lofty ideals but by being rooted and grounded in Christ by faith. The ideals they strove to realize had the "appearance of wisdom" but really they lacked any value because they were not truly God's ideals and were not motivated or carried out in His strength. These religious perfectionists in Colossae had given only their external lives to God and not their hearts and minds (Colossians 2:20–3:2). Paul said rather than religiously doing things to earn favor with God they needed to focus instead on being in a relationship with Christ by faith. They didn't need to fear not measuring up to the requirements of the law because through faith in Christ those requirements were fulfilled for them. They had been "raised with Christ" and had true life "hidden with Christ in God" (Colossians 3:1, 3). Paul said that they could discover this true life by putting off their old selves and ideals and putting on their new selves, which were the new creatures of ever-increasing glory that God was making them to be—a true ideal (Colossians 3:9, 10).

Kristi says that before we close this chapter I have to confess my own perfectionism! Like some of you and some of the Christians in ancient Colossae, I'm a perfectionist. I am less of one now than I used to be, though, and have overcome many of the effects of my perfectionism on my spiritual life. The way I've moved beyond the "spiritual shoulds," legalistic standards, and "super-me syndrome" of perfectionism is by emotionally redefining my image of God. I had to uncover the "false terrorist gods'' by taking the GIQ and begin the process of working through the layers of emotion surrounding my distorted God Images. Only such a brutal emotional honesty about our image of God can lay the foundation for discovering God's perfect love.

This is a process of emotionally redefining your image of God. For one man who entered therapy with a Christian psychologist this meant seeing God as Jesus who was like his mother rather than as a Heavenly Father who was like his dad.[14] He entered therapy feeling as if God had puppet strings on him and was always trying to force him to do things a certain way. This was how he felt toward his dad, whom he felt he could never please. By seeing God as ''my Jesus'' who was friendly and understanding like his mother this man improved his image of God.

This process of emotionally redefining our God Image can lead to some exciting things for perfectionists. First of all, instead of being enslaved by a Demanding Drill Sergeant God who keeps driving us we can spontaneously offer ourselves to the Real God who is considerate and loving. This enables us to be freed from serving God because we ''should'' and allows us to offer Him our love and service because we want to. Also we no longer fear an Outtagetcha Police Detective God who looks to trip us up but instead feel safe in the loving arms of the Real God that is ''Outtahelpya.'' Thus, instead of seeking to avoid getting caught making a mistake, we seek to do what is good (1 John 4:18; Romans 12:21). Third, we walk away from the false god of ''Absolute Perfection'' and walk toward the Real God of ''Absolute Acceptance.'' Rather than hiding our real selves underneath our ideal selves, we are able to entrust our real selves to God.

I often share with people who struggle with some aspect of religious perfectionism the ''mountain vision'' that God gave me. When my image of God was of a terrorist god, I used to imagine that in my prayer time I had to work up a spiritual sweat as I climbed my way up to the mountain of God. As I struggled my way up, I pulled up my excess baggage of guilt and imperfection. When I finally reached the top of the mountain,

God would fellowship with me and I could have a sense of satisfaction that I had made up for my inadequacies and made it to the top. To help me discover an accurate image of God's gracious love God gave me a new vision of this mountain scene while I was singing, "How lovely on the mountains is the feet of Him who brings good news . . . . Our God reigns . . . ." This time God didn't wait at the top of the mountain, watching me suffer as I tried to reach the top. Instead, God came down the mountain to get me, in the person of Jesus. Jesus picked me up and strapped me to His back so that I was the cross He carried. From on His back all that I could see were His feet, walking up the mountain. He brought to me the "good news" of God's grace, carrying me all the way to the top of the mountain to be with God. In my place He suffered the mocking and beatings of the people and was crucified on top of the mount at Calvary so that I could have relationship with God.

The good news is that we don't have to be perfect to please God because Christ was perfect for us. When we put our faith in Christ and our relationship with Him we are perfect in God's eyes!

Questions for Reflection and Discussion

1. What do Jesus' words "Be perfect" (Matthew 5:48) and Paul's words "Aim for perfection" (2 Corinthians 13:11) mean to you? Can you be perfect "in Christ" and aim for perfection without being perfectionistic, legalistic, or workaholic?

2. Read and react to the following three Scripture passages: (1) Philippians 2:12, 13: Paul says we are to work out our salvation as God works in us to will and to act. What does it mean to "work out" what God "works in"? (2) Ephesians 2:8–10: Paul says that God's grace leads us to do good works. How does receiving God's grace help us to do good works? (3) Hebrews 4:1–11: We are exhorted to "make every effort" to enter God's rest. How do you "work" at resting? What makes these concepts so hard for perfectionists and workaholics?

3. Are you more "doing" focused or more "being" focused? Would you say you are "results" oriented or "process" oriented? Do you

spend more energy on enhancing "external things" (i.e., appearance, accomplishments, possessions) or internal qualities?

4. Do you ever feel as if you need to earn "brownie points" or "atta boys" to win God's favor and blessing?

5. Meditate on the parable of the prodigal son in Luke 15:11–32. Put yourself in the prodigal's shoes. How would you feel if you failed your dad that way? How would your dad react? What if you failed your Heavenly Father? In your heart how do you imagine God would react? Do you identify with the perfectionistic older brother at the end of the story who was jealous that his brother would be given so much for doing nothing when the older brother had worked so hard for so long and felt that he never got rewarded?

6. Reflect on the "mountain vision" at the end of this chapter. In your life do you tend to work your way up the mountain to get to God? Or do you give up trying because you don't think you can make it? Or maybe you get impatient waiting at the bottom for God to get you and leave? Or do you get distracted and do other things? Can you see yourself patiently waiting at the bottom for Jesus to come get you and then letting Him carry you up to God?

8
Shhh! I'm Angry at God!

. . . My complaint is bitter; [God's] hand is heavy on me in spite of my groaning.

Job 23:2

When Job suddenly had his wealth stolen, most of his family killed, and was afflicted with painful boils, his wife said to him: ". . . Curse God and die!" (Job 2:9.) Job rejected this advice, recognizing that it was foolish to forsake his Almighty Creator and give up on life. Instead Job's initial response to his suffering was to accept it as being from God and having some purpose (Job 1:20–22; 2:10). When Job's misery did not let up he started to become angry at God because he felt hurt by Him. Job did not recognize that his anger was at God though, and in Job 3 we see that he made the mistake of turning his feelings of anger inward on himself and began to curse the day of his birth and condemn himself. He buried his anger inside himself rather than acknowledging that he was angry without sinning, as is the biblical ideal (Ephesians 4:26). His anger at God smoldered inside him until his life was darkened by gray smoke clouds of depression. Job's suffering did not cease and his anger at God continued to smolder inside him until it sparked into a raging fire of bitterness against God (Job 23:2). In his bitter anger against God, Job made the opposite mistake—explosively arguing and uncontrollably contending with God.

Job needed to understand that his anger was like a fiery hot coal that would burn his hands if he held on to it and start a destructive fire if he threw it. The Bible wisely advises us to put away all wrath quickly and be careful to be angry without sinning (Psalms 37:8; Ephesians 4:26). Job made the same mistake that many people I counsel make. He tried to push his anger back down inside himself. That's like trying to hold a beach ball underwater! And as you might guess, it was only a matter of time before the beach ball of Job's anger at God popped up from under the surface and exploded aggressively upward at God.

So at first Job was too passive and indirect with his anger and then he became too aggressive and out of control with it. Both extremes are a mishandling of anger. Anger needs to be acknowledged and properly expressed—even if that anger is at God! If we are brave enough, many of us would admit that once or twice we've felt a twinge of anger at God. But, if for you anger is a "no-no" then anger at God is a "NO-NO!" Like Job we may want to keep our anger a secret, because it is ugly; especially if the anger is at God.

I Can't Get Angry at God!

Most of us have grown up with strong social and religious taboos against expressing anger. As Pierre Wolff notes in his pointed little book *May I Hate God?*

> We often consider it bad to become angry or to hate, think that it is even worse to express such feelings, and that it would be

blasphemy to tell them to the Lord! And imagine the Lord being the target![1]

Lewis Smedes is a professor at Fuller Theological Seminary who has worked with people on the sticky issue of facing their negative feelings of anger and hate toward God in order to "forgive" Him. In his book *Forgive and Forget* he illustrates the importance of facing our anger at God by telling a story of a tailor, who is on the way out from his time of prayer in the synagogue and runs into a rabbi.

"Well, and what have you been doing in the synagogue, Lev Ashram?" the rabbi asks.

"I was saying prayers, rabbi."

"Fine, and did you confess your sins?"

"Yes, rabbi, I confessed my little sins."

"Your little sins?"

"Yes, I confessed that I sometimes cut my cloth on the short side, that I cheat on a yard of wool by a couple of inches."

"You said that to God, Lev Ashram?"

"Yes, rabbi, and more. I said, 'Lord, I cheat on pieces of cloth; you let babies die. But I am going to make you a deal. You forgive me my little sins and I'll forgive you your big ones.' "[2]

As Smedes notes, just as this Jewish tailor "grabbed ahold of God and held him to account," so we need to face our anger at God when we feel hurt by Him. Yet, just the thought of getting angry at God causes an automatic reaction of wanting to rush to defend God and defiantly and piously pronounce that God cannot be blamed for anything. Perhaps you're even questioning our wisdom in writing this chapter and trying to reassure yourself that God deserves to be protected from our ugly anger. After all, God is perfect and never does anything wrong so what right do we have to blame Him for anything? God certainly isn't responsible for our problems, is He? He is a God of love and wouldn't ever hurt us, would He?

Does the Almighty God really need to be defended and protected from our anger? The issue here is really our own discomfort with the thought of being angry at God. It's uncomfortable to be angry with anyone we love, especially God! We're afraid that our anger will break up our relationship with Him or cause further conflict. One woman said to me, "If I get angry at my husband he just gives me the silent treatment for days so I just don't let him see when I get angry. It's the same with God. I'm afraid He'll reject me and won't talk to me if I let Him see I'm angry." This woman was playing a game of hide-and-seek with God—trying to hide her anger from an Omniscient God. When I pointed out to her this silly game she was playing with God she said that she knew that He knew about her anger at Him, but she didn't want Him to *know* that she knew that He knew! Like some of us this woman was really hiding her anger at God from herself because she was afraid her anger would cause God to reject her.

Perhaps you've said to yourself, "Anger is a sin so I'm not going to get angry at anyone, especially God!" This is a popular misconception among Christians. Kristi and I once watched a minister on television preach about the evilness and ungodliness of anger. We had to laugh though because as he was preaching this sermon he often got red-faced and pounded his fist on the pulpit to make his point. He appeared to be angrily preaching at us! Some people would respond to this by saying there is "righteous indignation" and then there is "sinful anger." This seemingly noble distinction gives God and other "holier than thou" people the right to be angry if it can be justified as "holy anger." The rest of us though are left with no right to get angry even if we are unjustly hurt.

We don't want you to misunderstand our point here, as there certainly is anger that is right and anger that is wrong. We tell people who struggle with handling their anger in a Christian way that *right anger* is a normal emotional response to feeling hurt or injured. It may be self-protection or it may be discontent with an injustice. In either case, right anger means you avoid losing your temper, or you refrain from blaming others for your problems and you work through your angry feelings before they turn into bitterness or resentment. If you believe that it is never "right" for you to feel angry at an injustice done to you then you certainly will avoid getting angry at God at all costs.

The cost of avoiding anger is quite high, as Pierre Wolff points out.

> So often we have been told, on the social plane as well as the religious, that it is very serious to have such feelings [of anger] against ourselves, against others or against God. Since childhood we have been judged and condemned by the attitude of others until we do the same thing to ourselves. And if God has been presented to us as the Supreme Judge as well, where can we go, to whom can we turn? We cannot keep from feeling anger or hatred; the fact that we feel them makes us feel guilty: we condemn ourselves, other people and God condemn us! We reach a dead end and turn ceaselessly around in circles, caught between the feelings that are consuming us and the guilt that is crushing us.[3]

The only way out of this vicious circle of anger to guilt and back again is to honestly and lovingly express our feelings. We all experience hurt feelings over injustices done to us and anger is the normal and divinely implanted response that we have to feeling wronged or injured. When we stop ourselves from feeling and appropriately expressing this anger in a Christian way it's like pretending that we really weren't hurt. This, of course, leaves us vulnerable to be hurt again because we're unwilling to stand up and defend ourselves. Avoiding feelings of anger also precludes us from forgiving the offender and restoring the relationship because we're denying that we were wronged in the first place.

King David noted that the longer we repress feelings like anger the more our inner anguish actually increases (Psalms 39:2, 3). Our anger doesn't go away just because we repress it, but like the beach ball held under water, it gains more and more momentum until it pops up when we least expect it. Sometimes it explodes uncontrollably as Job's anger finally did. Other times it stays underground and disguises itself so that we can maintain the facade that we don't get angry.

I Don't Get Angry Anyway

Some people are convinced that they don't get angry at anyone and certainly not at God. They'll say, "It's foolish to get angry because it doesn't accomplish anything anyway." If it's foolish to get angry it's especially so to get angry at God because isn't He always right anyway? This is the attitude of one soft-spoken, mild-mannered husband I know. He said, "If I get angry at my wife she gets hysterical and cries and screams almost uncontrollably. Then things stay real uncomfortable until we can forget it." This man related to God as he related to his wife. Even when he felt hurt or mistreated he avoided appropriately expressing any angry feelings for fear that it would only make things worse. He neglected to work through the inevitable misunderstandings that occur in any relationship, especially one with an invisible God. Consequently, he often felt the same resentful and emotionally distant feelings toward God that he felt toward his wife.

People like this man disguise their anger in a stoic lack of feeling. They become numb to being emotionally wounded or violated by closing off their feelings. Their anger gets stuffed behind a wall of detachment and resentment. Such people may become like turtles hiding their heads inside hard protective shells so they won't get hurt. Or they may react the opposite way, like biting snakes, sure to attack and hurt others before others can hurt them. These people need to get in touch with and appropriately express their feelings if they're to have meaningful relationships with God and others.

Others of us repress the "right anger" we feel when we are treated unfairly or hurt by someone. It's as if we're subconsciously agreeing with the one who violated us: "I deserve to be hurt. I'm being treated as cheap and worthless because I am." This unhealthy attitude is a sign of repressed anger and is often disguised as depression, low self-esteem, or allowing yourself to be taken advantage of by others. The energy behind your anger gets bottled up inside so that even if you've been mistreated you don't have the "oomph" to stand up for yourself and face the issue. Sometimes, if we perceive God has hurt us or disappointed us, we even need to stand up to God and tell Him how we feel. Otherwise, we may hold a secret grudge against God or conclude that He treats us poorly.

Another way people subconsciously disguise their anger is by becoming supercontrolled so they never lose their temper. It's amazing how some people will try so hard to stay controlled and composed and to not get angry no matter what happens. This style of handling anger affects their relationship with God. One woman found that when she was completing the God Image Questionnaire she got in touch with her angry feelings at God. It was so uncomfortable for her to get angry that she stopped filling out the questionnaire (and stopped being honest with God) and put it away in a drawer to be forgotten with her anger.

A man, who also was angry at God, was composing a prayer in which he was asking God for financial help. He was trying to keep a lid on his anger, but the lid blew off as he scratched out the words *God, give me an answer!* He was so angry at God that it took him five tries just to write the *G* in *God.* Both of these people felt extremely anxious about letting themselves feel anger at God. So they fought to avoid dealing with their angry feelings and paid the price by sacrificing genuine closeness with God.

One woman I know never lets herself get angry. She says that anger is "unchristian." She has a lot to be angry about though, as she has a history of being abandoned time and again by those she loves. When she was three years old she was put in a foster home, never to see her real parents again. Then, shortly after they were married, her husband divorced her. What happens to the anger that must rage within her like a violent storm at sea? She doesn't acknowledge her inner rage at being abandoned. She certainly doesn't share her feelings with God since she believes anger is wrong. Frequently though, she has assorted physical problems. Headaches, feeling sick to her stomach, shooting neck pains, and a host of other ills plague her. Her body has to use up so much energy to contain her suppressed inner rage that its ability to function is weakened. Her submerged anger is a constant drain on her that leaves her stressed and tired. She knows this but hasn't yet been able to face her anger over being abandoned because she thinks God doesn't want her to have angry feelings.

We all get angry. It's just that we subconsciously disguise our anger. Disguising anger as emotional numbness, depression, or physical problems doesn't solve our problem. Jonah and Jeremiah were two prophets who both got angry at God and suffered from depression and other disguised forms of anger until they acknowledged this anger. Unresolved anger at God creates havoc on our fragile images of Him. I routinely find that people who are having problems in their relationship with God are secretly angry at Him. They can't receive healing in their relationship with God and in their image of Him without emotionally working through their anger in the company of God. "The healing process must include the courage to unmask the anger, bring it out before God, and put it on the cross where it belongs. There will be no healing until it is acknowledged, confronted, and resolved."[4]

The Real Problem Underneath Our Anger

Kristi and I live in Orange County, California, fifty miles outside of Los Angeles along the Saddleback Mountain Range. On a clear, cool, and breezy day in winter we have a beautiful view of this graceful and majestic mountain range from our second-floor balcony. However, in the summer when it's hot and there is no wind it sometimes gets so smoggy that we can barely see Saddleback Mountain.

We are both nature lovers, so in the smoggy summers we often feel angry and cheated by the smog-covered mountains. Yet, in the winter when the air is clear we have the opposite reaction of admiration toward the same mountain.

In the same way, many people have opposite reactions of anger and adoration at the Creator of the mountains. When we get angry at God we're really getting angry at the smog of our distorted God Images which is hiding His love from us. If we face our angry feelings at God we'll see that underneath we feel hurt by an oppressive false god. Instead of denying our anger and choking the breath of God within us in the smog, we need to allow the cool winds of the Spirit of Love to blow away our smoggy images of God so that we see Him as He really is.

When we've felt hurt or let down by God it's normal to feel anger at Him. Again and again in the Psalms we see David and the other Psalmists expressing feelings that God has failed them in some way. Instead of bypassing their anger and stuffing their painful feelings, the Psalmists use their anger in a healthy way by going straight to God, confronting the issue of how they feel toward Him, and even questioning Him.

Bud, who was struggling with anger at God, decided to take my advice and write his own "angry psalm" to God:

> I have resentment, anger, and mistrust for you God. Sometimes I can feel it come up when I read the Bible or pray to you. I can feel it now while writing this. I don't want it. I don't feel it's okay to feel it. I don't really know where it started. Somewhere as a child. Maybe also from identifying with the pain of others, the pain and injustice in the world. I can remember way back feeling confusion and anger at the pain and injustice I see around me. The old question, God, if You are so good and powerful why do You let all this pain happen?

Like the Psalmists in the Bible, Bud faced his anger and brought it to God. Because Bud was honest and direct with his anger at God he was able to get to the real issue underneath his anger. He felt hurt and disappointed by God over all the painful and unjust things that had happened to him.

God meant for anger to signal to us that there is a problem within us or in a relationship that needs attention. When we deny our angry feelings by repressing them or make the opposite mistake of losing control and blowing up, we make our anger a problem. Then we have two problems—our inner wound and our mishandled anger that has caused further injury to ourselves or someone else. Usually the latter problem arises out of the former; we lose our temper because we've got so much anger boiling over within us. We saw how this is what happened to Job. He turned his anger at God inward, disguising it as self-condemnation and depression. Then he couldn't contain his anger any longer and he exploded at God, which only ended in a fight that he had no chance of winning! Meanwhile, Job was not giving enough attention to the real issue, which was his hurt feelings at a mean and vicious caricature of God. Within him was an emotional wound that would not just go away or be healed with the passing of time.

Job's real problem was that he felt deeply hurt that God would take away all his wealth, kill his family, and afflict him with a devastating disease. Job was caught in the human dilemma of looking at God "through a glass, darkly" and consequently he saw an imperfect and clouded picture of Him (1 Corinthians 13:12 KJV). In the midst of his suffering he developed negative perceptions of God as his "opponent" who "shattered," "tormented," "crushed," "attacked," "wronged," and "stripped" him of his honor (Job 16:9, 12; 19:2, 3, 6, 9). Job imagined God was stalking him like a hungry lion waiting to attack a helpless baby bird in its nest (Job 10:16). He couldn't escape this vicious god and he certainly couldn't defend himself.

Yet, God didn't cause all this destruction; Satan was clearly the agent of evil (Job 1:9–12; 2:4–6). God did allow Job to suffer, though, and certainly didn't back down from taking responsibility for Job's suffering (Job 2:3). What Satan meant for evil, God meant for good, for God works all things together for the good of those who love Him (Genesis 50:20; Romans 8:28). In the end, Job finally realized that all his suffering was actually for his own personal good. God restored to Job all that he ever had and much more. Job was a better and happier man for what he had gone through. Perhaps his experience of suffering wouldn't have been so unbearable, if he could have grasped the divine and eternal perspective in the midst of his tragedy. If only in faith Job could have hung on to a more accurate image of his Loving God and seen God's benevolent purpose in Job's suffering.

In counseling with Christians Kristi and I have found this challenge that Job faced to be the most difficult issue for them. Like Job many people feel abandoned, let down, or hurt by God in the midst of their suffering. Not seeing things through the eyes of eternity, they develop a twisted and negative perception of God. When our God Image is a distorted image of a harsh or uncaring "Divine Disappointment," it's no wonder we feel hurt by Him and get mad at Him. It is the pain of these negative God Images that are the real issue underneath our anger at God. We shouldn't be surprised if we occasionally feel anger at God even though we love Him so much. Those we love the most are the ones who have the greatest likelihood of hurting us. It is no exception with God. We love and need Him more than anyone else in our lives. We depend on Him for everything. When things seem to go amiss and He isn't there for us or hurts us somehow, it is a catastrophic disappointment that's likely to arouse a twinge of anger. This anger really isn't at God as much as it is at our limited and distressful picture of Him in our hearts.

Wrestling With God

Instead of hiding the occasional misunderstandings, disagreements, and conflicts that inevitably arise in our relationship with God we need to talk to God about how we feel.

> If we listen attentively to our hearts, to the cries of our friends and our angry world, we may find ourselves in conflict with God. We believe in a God who is mercy and justice, yet we see so much injustice. We believe in a God who is wholeness and salvation,

> yet we see so much brokenness and suffering. We believe in a God of love, yet we see so much hatred. These conflicts raise questions. And to ask these questions not as academic riddles but as life demands is to wrestle with God.[5]

To honestly confront God with our questions and complaints is to wrestle with Him. Some may view such angry protests as a lack of faith. In some cases, perhaps they are. In many cases though, they are actually a sign of deep faith. This was the case for Jacob, who wrestled with God and prevailed (Genesis 32:22–32); for Job, who practically fought with God and afterward was prospered beyond measure; and for David, who often confronted God in the Psalms and was called a man after God's own heart. Some life circumstances demand that we struggle with God in order to get to the bottom of things. To wrestle with God in order to resolve our anger over pain and injustice proves the depth of our trust in God and reflects our commitment to a truly honest, real, and intimate relationship with Him.

A friend of mine wrestled with God to resolve his anger at Him. From his perspective, God seemed like a "Holy Terror" out to bring pain and misery. He complained, "When I found out my wife had a recurrence of cancer I felt as if God had slugged me and knocked the wind out of me. I was gasping for air . . . why? Haven't we suffered enough?" My friend felt knocked down by God, but he courageously got up and confronted God with his questions.

A girl Kristi counseled was also mad at God. She said, "I told God He is like a Sadistic Potter who molded me into a cruel joke! Why did He make me into a big, fat, and ugly pot? He made me to be a trash container under the sink when I wanted to be a pretty vase on the mantel with flowers in it! I want to trust God, but it doesn't seem like He made me to be anything special."

I ran into another example of someone wrestling with God when I read the bizarre case study of an eleven-year-old boy's image of God.[6] He was angry at God because he had an image of God as a harsh judge who criticized his faults and forced him to deny himself the things he wanted. His anger at God got out of control when he stabbed a picture of Jesus with a knife until it was mutilated! Then he locked the picture in a desk drawer.

Symbolically, this boy was acting out his anger at God and locking God out of his heart. His way of wrestling with God went from a vicious display of anger to an obstinate avoidance of God. Years later, after a rebellious adolescence in which he stayed as far away from church as he could, he happened upon the mutilated picture of Jesus. Seeing what he had done enabled him to reexamine his feelings from a new perspective. He realized that he had projected his own harsh and judgmental conscience onto a Loving God and so recommitted his life to Christ.

Other people angrily wrestle with God because He feels distant in time of need. Usually this sounds something like, "Where were You, God, when I needed You?" Indeed, sometimes God's love seems farthest away when we need it most. At such times, God's apparent absence may feel like a "Divine Disappointment" that leaves you angry. One young man was angry at a twisted caricature of a "Tightwad God" who was closefisted and withheld the things the young man needed. He complained to God, "Was it too much to ask, Lord? Why didn't you give me the scholarship I needed? You could have helped me pay for school, but instead I have to work an extra job just to make ends meet." Other common Divine Disappointments are the Statue God, who is cold and distant; the Indian Giver God, who backs out when you need Him; the Preoccupied Managing Director God, who is too busy to give you any attention; and the Marshmallow God, who is too weak to protect you. They're all mistaken views of God. Many people experience God as being so small and unhelpful that it's no wonder they feel hurt by Him and react with hidden anger.

Dealing With Anger at God

The proper way to handle anger is modeled for us again and again in some of the Psalms. Because of the negative and sinful connotations of anger, theologians have disguised these angry Psalms by calling them "Imprecatory Psalms." Although we don't talk much about these Psalms, if you look carefully you will see that they are full of angry feelings.[7] In the most graphic displays of anger David asks God to break his enemies' arms, cut off their lips and tongues, tear out their teeth, and even to blot their names out of the book of life (Psalms 10:15; 12:3; 58:6; 69:28). In verses like these David acknowledges his anger at those who have hurt him, records his angry feelings in a prayer to God, entrusts his anger to God by asking Him to bring vengeance, and believes that God will ultimately heal his wounds and deliver him (*see* chapter 10 for further discussion of the pattern of dealing with feelings presented in Psalms). This is far more healthy than burying your anger or seeking revenge yourself. This kind of emotional honesty—"truth in the inner parts" as David sought in Psalms 51:6—restores fellowship and intimacy with our best friend, our Abba Father in heaven.

Not only is a right handling of anger modeled for us in the Psalms, but our Lord Jesus Himself shows us that it's okay to get angry for the right reason. He was obviously quite angry when He turned over tables and drove out the people who were misusing God's temple (Matthew 21:12, 13). Also, on a number of occasions, Jesus' anger at the self-righteousness of the Pharisees was apparent. He was so angry that He referred to them as snakes, hypocrites, and children of the devil (Matthew 23:28–33; John 8:44). In Jesus' sermon on the mount He gave us some wise words about anger. It's not good to be angry without cause, but if you do deal with your anger wrongly, seek forgiveness. When you have cause to be angry deal with it quickly, but do deal with it because if you don't it will imprison you (Matthew 5:21–26).

We would all be wise to listen to Jesus' words and to follow David's example of dealing with anger rightly. If your anger is at God then it is all the more important to acknowledge it, express the feelings in a proper way, and in faith ask God to help you separate His true loving nature from your imperfect perceptions of Him. Remember that God is big enough to handle your feelings of anger at Him. If you're honest with all your feelings and listen to His response you'll see that He really does love you even though sometimes it might not seem like it.

Questions for Reflection and Discussion

1. Read Psalms 37:8 and Ephesians 4:26. Do you believe it's a sin to get angry? What if that anger is at God? In your opinion what is the difference between "right anger" and "wrong anger"?

2. What's your reaction to the story of Job? Was he being punished for his sin? Did he suffer because he feared it happening in the first place (Job 3:25)? Was he being disciplined by God? Was it an attack from Satan? In the end was God disappointed in the way Job handled his suffering? What did Job do right in the way he responded to his suffering? What could he have done better? How do you react to suffering?

3. Do you ever get angry? If you avoid getting angry, how do you disguise your anger (depression, low self-esteem, emotional numbness, physical problems)? If you get angry, how do you express it (losing your temper, quiet resentment, subtle revenge, your blocking out feelings)?

4. Think of your closest relationship with either your spouse, best friend, or a parent. In that relationship, how do you deal with conflict (ignore, resolve immediately, explode, put off resolving it until later, try to "fix" the problem, talk out your feelings and negotiate differences through understanding each other)? Now think about your relationship with God. Are there any similarities?

5. What do you think about the idea of wrestling with God when you're angry at Him? Is it okay to confront, question, argue with, or complain to God? If you don't ever wrestle with God how do you deal with misunderstandings, disagreements, or conflicts you might have with Him?

6. Have you ever been angry at God? How did you express or disguise your anger at God? What was your image of God at that time?

9 Seeing a New Image of God

Blessed is the man who makes the Lord his trust, who does not . . . turn aside to false gods.

Psalms 40:4

So far you've learned about the importance of your God Image to spiritual maturity and emotional well-being. You've also seen some of the mistaken God Images people develop and why they negatively distort God's love in these ways. Additionally, you've discovered the hidden troubling feelings many people have in their relationship with God. You may even have uncovered some of your own distorted images of God that need work. But in all this you've only gotten a hint of how you can improve your perception of God to see a more loving image of Him. This is the crux of the whole issue. If you're aware of having any distressful God Images and are wondering how to overcome them, then your question is: ''So where do I go from here?''

Where Do We Go From Here?

That is what one middle-aged coupled asked. The calm and insistent manner behind their question was surprising. This couple had stored up resentments and anger toward each other for years, and it all came out at once when they came for counseling.

They were slinging mud at each other week after week, digging up unresolved conflicts that had been buried years earlier. Resentment and bitterness had piled up until they were about to get a divorce. They had to face their unpleasant feelings. Indeed, it was high time they finally threw the mud they'd been living in! When they finally asked what to do next, we were able to bring in a hose and clean up the mess they'd uncovered.

You're probably just as ready to bring out that water hose so you can wash away any muddy God Images you've uncovered. You want more than anything to know God's love in personal experience and to help others do the same. Yet, just like this married couple, it's easy to keep burying the troubled and hurt feelings you experience in your relationship with God until you've buried yourself in a spiritual tomb. If you've buried any negative feelings toward God then they need to be unearthed and talked about. A first it may seem that you're needlessly wrestling around with God in a pit of mud, but once all the mud is thrown you'll be ready to be hosed off in God's love. Mistaken images of God can be ugly and dirty, but the only way to be free of them is to bring them out into the open and deal with them.

Many Christians don't like to bring things out into the open. They tend to be very secretive about their relationship with God. They want to be helped without opening up the wounds that need to be cleaned. They want to overcome their problems without climbing the wall that is blocking their way. They want a quick fix, a spiritual pill to take away their pain, a magical erasure to erase their negative God Images. This translates into wishful thinking that a minister's prayer, a certain Bible verse, a special sermon, or the right seminar will be the final cure-all. None of these easy remedies is likely to have a substantial impact on helping them overcome troubling images of God.

There must be an emotional healing of past wounds. Ingrained and habitual patterns of living and of relating to others need to be changed. This type of change cannot occur unless one is willing to go through some pain and struggle. It takes time to change negative images of God that have taken years to develop. What we are talking about here is more a process of emotional healing than simply intellectual insight. It's something that is more likely to take place in the context of loving relationships than informational teachings.

Christian ministers and workers must understand this need to work through problems on a feeling and relational level. Unfortunately, some people have been sorely disappointed by insensitive and simplistic answers to their problems from untrained helpers. One man went to see a lay counselor who tried to solve the man's feelings of insecurity by quoting Scripture and giving him a pat on the back. This man didn't feel understood or loved and received no help on the emotional level where he needed it.

A woman feeling abandoned by God went to see her pastor. But the pastor didn't have time to listen to her and wasn't trained to counsel, so he prayed for her and sent her away without referring her to a professional Christian counselor. This woman also didn't feel cared for and received no help with her distressful God Image. Overcoming troubled God Images and other emotional difficulties requires more than a few Bible verses, a prayer, a sermon, or a pat on the back. In many cases, such problems won't even be solved by better doctrine, more regular church attendance, improved Bible study, or increased prayer.

What will help? How can you overcome distressful God Images? In chapter 3 we said that the source of our struggles to perceive and experience God's love is in hurtful interpersonal relationships. Usually, there is a specific painful experience, a collection of such experiences, or a pattern of troubled relationships that is the source of distorted God Images. Agnes Sanford deals with these issues in a form of therapy that she calls the healing of memories or the forgiveness of sins (your own sins or the sins of others against you). She notes the importance of a loving relationship in this process by saying, "There are in many of us wounds so deep that only the mediation of someone else to whom we may 'bare our grief' can heal us."[1] This healing process must address the emotional traumas and patterns of thinking and acting that resulted from past relationships. Otherwise, the troubled person's doctrinal belief system about God will remain divorced from his personal experience of God.

Helping someone truly overcome distressful God Images requires the involvement of the person's whole self in a comprehensive treatment plan. A real change in distressful God Images occurs when each mode of functioning (doing/relating, feeling, thinking, motivation, and perception) is taken into account and personal, interpersonal, and spiritual resources are utilized (*see* diagram on page 148). This includes the following five steps:

1. Acknowledge and confess to another person any negative God Images you have.
2. Share related feelings with someone you trust and in a personal prayer journal.
3. Study Scriptures affirming the aspects of God's love you struggle to receive.
4. Pray (and be prayed for) that God would supernaturally enable you to receive His perfect love.
5. Meditate on biblical pictures of God as loving and yourself as lovable.

Getting Started

In any area of desired personal or spiritual growth the first thing you need to do is admit your need. This is the road of humility. You walk on this road by taking action and seeking help from people you trust. To do this and really share your spiritual hurts and struggles with someone else requires a bold

OVERCOMING THE IMPACT OF DISTORTED GOD IMAGES ON PERSONALITY

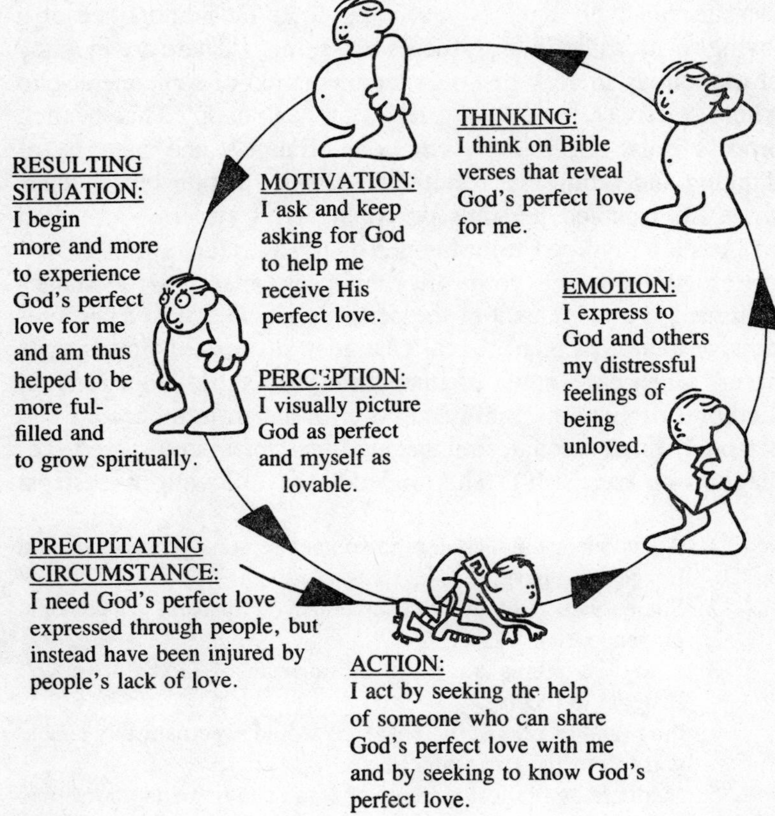

and brave emotional honesty. Only then can the two of you go through the discomfort of confronting your negative images of God and bringing them out from the dark corners of your subconscious. One woman who sought help said, "It's really hard for me to ask you to pray for me. I was taught to handle things on my own and not ask for any help." Although it was hard to be vulnerable, it was the best way for her to develop a more positive and loving image of God.

If you've read each of the preceding chapters then you've already begun this process. Through sharing the painful experiences of the people in these pages and completing the God Image Questionnaire (GIQ), you've likely uncovered some of your own negative images of God. You've surely been able to identify with some of the people described. Whatever your personal struggles with God are find someone you trust to share them with. There is something about sharing your difficulties with another person that is healing. Let this other person—whether he or she is a friend, spouse, small group leader, pastor, or counselor—be God's ambassador to you. This person will be a representative of Christ's love and can serve as the rickety old bridge from your old, negative images of God to new and positive God Images. Indeed, we all need someone to be our discipler; someone to model and express God's love to us, and someone to lead us in our journey. As A. W. Tozer says, "When we try to imagine what God is like we must of necessity use that which is not God as the raw material for our minds to work on."[2]

If your helper is mature, he or she can minister to you the specific aspects of God's love that are hardest for you to receive. Ideally, a helper will provide for you a loving and safe relationship that can serve as a backdrop for you to receive healing prayer and divine insight into your personality. A healing interpersonal relationship like this will enable you to emotionally differentiate the Loving God from people in your past who have been less than perfectly loving toward you and maybe even wounded you emotionally. For until you have concretely and practically experienced God's love firsthand from other people, it will be almost impossible for you to know God's love at a deeper level than intellectually and doctrinally. This is why it is so important that Christians love one another. We are God's eyes, ears, hands, and feet to one another. I see God's tears of compassion for me in your tears for me. You feel the warmth of His hug when I embrace you. In doing this we give one another a cup of cold water in Jesus' name.

Dealing With Feelings

I was at the dentist's office the other day getting a cavity filled. The dentist leaned over and said, "This is going to hurt!" I replied, "That's okay as long as it's pain with a purpose." I can manage painful feelings that come in the process of reaching a goal I've set. It's meaningful pain because it is a necessary part of a larger purpose. It's hopeful pain because I know things will get better. I didn't mind the pain of having my tooth drilled to fill a cavity, just as I don't mind the emotional pain I need to go through to grow spiritually. In both cases the pain has meaning and hope. When people don't have this meaning and hope they kick and scream in the dentist's chair or try to stay away from the dentist altogether. In other areas of life these people do the same thing: When they sit in life's chair, they either cry out to be rescued from their pain, or they act as if they don't have any feelings at all so no one will know they hurt. In either case they don't have meaning and hope in their pain so they neglect to work through the negative feelings that inevitably arise in their relationships with other people and with God.

Once we become aware of our need and acknowledge that we have some negative images of God, the next step is to express the feelings that make up our God Image. It is so important to express these feelings we have in our relationship with God. None of us has a perfect relationship with God. At one time or another we all feel that God is distant, uncaring, overly demanding, or disappointing in some way. We've already talked about how many of the great leaders in the Bible confronted and worked through negative feelings toward God. Job, David, Solomon, and Jeremiah serve as examples of a biblical way of dealing with negative feelings toward God and others. Even Jesus worked through negative feelings in His life, particularly at Golgotha. Yet, despite these examples, the Christian church as a whole today neglects feelings. For most Christians the emotional component of their spirituality is severely underdeveloped. We tend to hide all our negative emotions behind sterile doctrines and rationalized beliefs. It's no wonder so many Christians have troubled emotional images of God hidden in their subconscious mind!

A young mother asked, "What do I do when I feel that God's love is far from me? I don't know what to do when I feel hurt or disappointed by Him or even angry at Him. How can I share with God these feelings that He doesn't seem to care about me?" When we went over some Psalms that expressed feelings of anger, depression, and doubt in God's love, she was shocked. "I thought all the Psalms were praises and songs of joy," she remarked in disbelief. This woman was relieved when she realized that it is okay to have negative feelings and that she could form them into a prayer to God. She started writing her own psalms to God in a journal. Some were psalms of thanks or praise and others were psalms of sorrow, anxiety, or anger. All were prayers to God.

You can write your own psalms just as this young mother did. This will help you deal with the negative feelings connected with distorted God Images. Try to follow a simple three-step pattern that was frequently used by David and the other Psalmists. First, address God. You might praise or thank Him or you may need to cry out to Him for help, question Him as to why He seems so distant and uncaring, or tell Him that you feel like He has forgotten you. Whether it's praise, an offering of thanks, a petition, a question, or a statement, the point is to honestly address God and make contact with Him according to what your needs are at the time. Second, express your feelings to God. These may be positive feelings of love, joy, peace, or trust. They may also be negative feelings of hate, anger, anxiety, sorrow, fear, or guilt. The idea is to be honest about your inner feelings and put them on paper in your prayer journal.

The third step to writing your own psalm is to respond to your feelings in faith. This is easy if you're praising God and you're full of joy. You just say something like, "I know Lord that You are good and loving and will continue to show me Your goodness and love." If you are recording a psalm of petition or questions and it's full of negative feelings then it's a little more of a challenge to respond in faith. You can respond to negative feelings in faith by saying something like, "Even though it feels like You've hidden Your face from me, I trust that You hear my prayers and will stretch out Your hand to save me."

When people are able to do this they are greatly helped emotionally and they also grow closer to God. One woman came for counseling because she was sexually abused as a child by her father's best friend. She felt angry at God and was convinced that He didn't care about her. Her perception of God was of a Pushy Salesman God—a Divine Disappointment. After a few weeks of creating her own psalms she began to trust God and was able to receive His comfort and love in the course of her therapy. Similarly, the emotional aspects of your spiritual life need attention. Writing your own psalms is a great way to deal with your feelings effectively and biblically. If you study the Psalms closely, you'll discover that many follow this pattern of addressing God, honestly expressing feelings, and responding in faith. Try it and see if in time you don't feel better and grow closer to God.

Renew Your Mind in Scripture

In step one you took an action step of humbly acknowledging your need and seeking help from someone. In step two you honestly expressed your feelings to your helper and to God. Now, in step three, you need to change your negative thought patterns. For most people this is the easiest step once they understand what is involved.

People who have distorted God Images not only tend to hide their images of God and to feel bad, but they also have negative thoughts about God and sometimes about themselves and others. One adolescent boy who was about ready to abandon his faith in Christ was full of negative thinking. A tape of his thoughts would have revealed something like, *God doesn't care about me. It's no use for me to pray or seek His help because He never responds anyway. Nobody really cares about me. Like my dad says, "I'll never amount to anything."* One of the things this boy could do to help himself was to change his thinking. Like most people with distorted God Images he had a problem with negative self-talk.

According to psychologist David Stoop, *self-talk* is what we say to ourselves. It consists of the stream of thoughts that constantly run through our minds at a rate as high as 1,300 words per minute.[3] Our self-talk has a great deal to do with how we feel toward God. If we fill our minds with negative thoughts about how we're afraid God won't answer our prayers and isn't concerned about our needs, then we'll feel let down and disappointed by God. This kind of negative spiritual self-talk is the breeding ground for false God Images. To reverse the effects of bad self-talk, people need to renew their minds in Scripture and reassure themselves of God's perfect love for them. By thinking about scriptural affirmations of God's patience, fairness, compassion, active kindness, and so on, they can help to increase their faith and trust in a Loving God and in the process feel better about themselves and their lives. In the next chapter we'll talk more about this and I'll show you how to use the "Eye Chart" to improve your spiritual self-talk and renew your God Image.

Prayer for a New Heart

In this fourth step to an improved God Image you'll use the discipline of prayer to renew your motivation to receive God's love. This step is similar to step two in that prayer is utilized and feelings and motivations are closely related. It's different in that your prayers are focused less on your troubled feelings and more on your unmet needs.

We all need to be loved and are motivated in various ways to meet that need. We need to be loved by people, but ultimately what we need most is to be loved perfectly by God. Underlying whichever of the fourteen false God Images you struggle with are some unmet needs for love. If you don't remember which of the fourteen aspects of God's love you have the most difficulty with, refer back to the God Image Questionnaire at the end of chapter 1 to identify your mistaken images of God and the corresponding aspects of God's perfect love that get distorted. You need to focus your prayer life on receiving these specific aspects of God's love (just as you need to focus your Scripture study on those same aspects in step three above). For instance, if your image of God is that of an Indian Giver false god then you especially need to experience God's steadfast love that is consistent, unfailing, and always keeps its promises.

What you should pray is that God would supernaturally express these aspects of His perfect love to you. You need to pray not only specifically, but also persistently. In Jesus' teaching on prayer in Luke 11:1–13, He said that we have not because we ask not and that we would receive good gifts from God to meet our needs if we ask Him and keep on asking Him for what we need. You need to persevere in your prayers to overcome the distorted God Images that leave you with unmet love needs. That's not easy, because you're trying to change a problem that likely took years to develop. If you don't give up in your specific prayers of faith, God will begin to bring healing. As you pray you'll become aware of what makes it so hard for you to receive those particular aspects of God's love. Best of all, you'll become more open to receiving the love from God that you need.

Meditation on Biblical Images of God

In this fifth and final step to improve your image of God you deal with the root of your problem—your perceptual images of

God. These images are inner pictures lodged in the emotional center of your subconscious mind. If you're like most people then probably a few of your images of God are significant distortions of the true and Loving God. Through the practice of meditation you can bring a false image of God into your conscious mind and have it renewed to be more like a true image of the Loving God.

In other words, if you have a false image of the Statue God who never moves to help you, you might meditate on the picture of God as an actively loving Shepherd who cares for and guides His precious sheep. This will help you begin to see God as active in your life and wanting to supernaturally intervene to help you. As your image of God is renewed by pictures of His love, you will grow closer to Him and feel better as well.

Some Christians have trouble with this step because they're afraid of the word *meditate*. They think that since some Eastern religious cults and non-Christian groups practice meditation it must be wrong. Yet, meditation, like prayer, Bible study, or worship, is only a tool or vehicle to accomplish a certain purpose. In itself, meditation is not good or bad. Whether it is good or not depends on its purpose. Relating with and glorifying Christ are the purposes of Christian meditation and that makes it valuable.[4] Unfortunately, even with this distinction in mind, some Christians are still unsure of whether or not meditation is biblical. They want Christianity to be a religion of reason and intellect only. They shy away from the emotional, experiential, and visual nature of meditation. Yet, if our Christianity doesn't include our feelings and our imaginations then we become like robots with big heads and no hearts.

Meditation is an important Christian discipline that is referred to several times in the Bible. It has been practiced by God-fearing men and women since the beginning of time. We're all familiar with Psalm 23 and David's poetic imagery. Have you ever thought of that as being an example of one of David's personal meditations on relating with God? In Psalm 23, David is imagining that he is like a sheep and God is like his shepherd. This is illustrative of many truths that, if pictured and meditated on at a feeling level, can help you develop a more biblical and loving God Image. The shepherd feels and cares for his sheep, guides them on the right path, protects them with his rod and staff, is with them in the valley of the shadow of death, and heals their wounds with his oil.

Psalm 23 is just one example of the many pictorial portions of Scripture that were likely written as meditations. The Bible is full of visual illustrations of what God is like and how He relates to us. I find it very helpful to meditate on some of these pictures of God in the Bible. Depending upon the individual's personal struggles I tell them to put themselves in a particular picture in Scripture. As they do this, their image of God and of themselves improves. They begin to truly experience God's love for them.

For instance, at the end of chapter 5, I suggested that people with feelings of inadequacy meditate on Jesus' picture of the loving father embracing the prodigal son who had failed miserably. Also, in chapter 6, I shared the story of how the man who had difficulty trusting God was helped by meditating on Psalm 91 where God is pictured as a nurturing and cuddly mother hen that provides a safe nest for her young chicks.

I used another meditation with a young woman of twenty-four who was having trouble getting up the courage to leave home and live on her own. In Deuteronomy 32, Moses uses the picture of God as like a mother eagle that cares for its young and then one day kicks the little eaglet out of the nest! The mother eagle then teaches her eaglet how to fly by repeatedly dropping and catching the little one. The eaglet learns to fly by trial and error and by its mother's example of flapping her wings as she hovers over the eaglet. This woman imagined herself in this picture and saw God helping her to live on her own. She prepared herself for the shock of falling through midair and discovered that even after she learned to fly on her own, God would always be right beside her. Drawing from Isaiah 40 she was able to picture God as the wind that gave her the strength to fly. This meditation helped her develop a more positive image of God. She was able to trust God because she began to feel His loving respect for her. He knew that she could fly and He was willing to teach her!

There are many pictures of God in the Bible that can be useful tools for renewing your image of God through meditation. Some others are potter and clay, refiner and gold, farmer and wheat, vine and branches, master and servant, and daddy and little child. Each of these illustrations contains truths about God's loving character and your lovableness. They can be meditated on to help you develop a more loving image of God. This will then help you feel better and more lovable and enable you to more effectively love God and others. (Some of these pictures of God that I've mentioned are discussed in the Questions for Reflection and Discussion at the end of each chapter.)

So if you're tired of wrestling with God and you want to hose off the dirt on your God Image there are some things you can do. You can see a more loving image of God by emotionally differentiating Him from the people who have hurt you in your past. You may need to do some forgiving, receive emotional healing, or discover new ways of relating with others. This will involve humbly acknowledging your difficulty and being open and vulnerable with people you trust and respect. These people can then help you to receive God's love in a new and deeper way so that you grow to personally know the God of love in whom you believe.

Additionally, there are some specific things you can do in your personal devotional life. Memorizing and confessing Scriptural promises of God's love, writing your own psalms, praying that God will help you to receive His love, and meditating on biblical pictures of your Loving God. Each of these steps will be most effective if you focus on one or two specific false images of God that you struggle with. One last thing you can do is learn the A-B-C's of your God Image.

Questions for Reflection and Discussion

1. Do you agree that right doctrine and good theology are not enough to significantly improve distressful God Images? Why or why not?

2. Who are the ambassadors in your life? To whom are you an ambassador? What are the benefits and what are the dangers of seeing certain people as representatives of what God is like?

3. How might your image of God influence your prayer life? For instance, what if you perceive God as distant from you, unconcerned about details, not intervening miraculously in your life, uncaring, having overly high expectations, wanting your prayers to be prayed in a certain way, only answering your prayers if you "deserve" the answer, or willing to grant your every wish if you follow the right formula?

4. What does *prayer* mean to you? Commonly, prayer is petitioning God, interceding for another, or thanking and praising God for things. Also important to prayer is sharing your feelings and struggles with God. (For instance see David's prayers in Psalm 13 and Psalms 25:16–22.) Try writing out a psalm of prayer to God in which you express to God any troubled feelings you have and then respond to your feelings in faith. How might this dimension of prayer affect your God Image?

5. Pick a Bible verse that is particularly meaningful to you. What is the impact of this verse on your image of God? Commit this verse to memory and then reflect on it during a time when you're struggling to really feel God's love for you.

6. From a Christian perspective, what does *meditation* mean to you? For some people it is restricted to thinking about a Scripture passage. How about bringing your whole self to a passage of Scripture by pondering its meaning for you, picturing any events or images that are described, observing your own feelings that are evoked, relating the Scripture to your personal struggles, and listening to what God speaks to your heart? Try meditating this way on Jesus' parable of the Sower in Matthew 13:3–9, 18–23. Picture God as a Farmer who prepares the ground of your heart, sows good seed into your life, waters your heart, and reaps a harvest from your life. What specific "good seeds" (gifts, abilities, and attributes) has God invested in you? What does your answer to this last question say about your image of God? Which of the four soils mentioned in Matthew 13 would best represent your response to the gifts God has sown in your life?

10
The A-B-C's of a Loving God Image

May it be the real Thou that I speak to; may it be the real me that speaks.

C. S. Lewis

For parents one of the highlights of raising a child is hearing him recite his A-B-C's for the first time. Once a child has accomplished this, you know that before long he'll be reading and writing his way into adulthood! There is another set of A-B-C's that is a little tougher to learn. As a matter of fact, many adults I run into haven't yet learned these A-B-C's! The A-B-C's they need to learn are part of the spiritual language we use to communicate with God. If we don't know the letters of the divine alphabet it's hard to understand what God is saying when He writes on the blackboard of life. It's in the midst of this confusion that we develop distorted God Images. The God of infinite love becomes just another letdown. We misread the blackboard to say

Santa Claus, Scrooge, Statue, Drill Sergeant, Party Pooper, or some other confused caricature of God. If we learn our A-B-C's we'll see quite clearly that the blackboard reads *Jesus, your loving Lord.*

Learning Your A-B-C's

Once we learn our A-B-C's it becomes easier to decipher divine handwriting. We discover the real messages in the various circumstances and experiences we encounter on life's journey. When we know more clearly what God is saying to us we can give Him a more appropriate response. This protects us from getting our feet caught in our mouths as Job did. If you recall our earlier discussion of Job, you'll remember that he became bitterly angry at God. Job accused God of being a deceitful enemy, an opponent who was like a vicious lion waiting to attack and torment him (Job 10:16). In the end, after Job had lashed out in anger against God, he was silenced by the righteous love of the One who was with him in his suffering and who restored Job to a place of abundant blessing. Job's distorted God Images masked the Real God of love. It wasn't until after his trial was over that Job realized he had subconsciously masked God in a crude Halloween costume! Job learned the A-B-C's of a true image of God the hard way.

To help avoid Job's mistake, allow me to play the part of ''professor of piety'' for a moment and teach you the A-B-C's of a loving God Image.

A: Activating event → B: Belief about God → C: Consequences

The first thing you need to learn is that you cannot avoid the *activating events* you bump into. No matter how hard you try, you can't avoid getting bumped and banged in the bumper-car game of life. From time to time, we all get hit by traumatic circumstances and unfortunate stresses. People who say Job could have avoided the suffering that befell him are fooling themselves. There is no such thing as life without pain and bruises. We can't control what happens to us at "A." But we can control the way that we respond to what happens to us at point "A."

Our response is noted at point "B" and reflects our *beliefs* or perceptions about God. Don't let the word *belief* fool you. I am not referring to your conscious thoughts about God, but the emotionally charged spiritual perceptions that become fixed in subconscious beliefs about God. Your response to the different activating events you bump into is not as much a matter of a doctrinal creed as it is a matter of style of worship. It is at the "B" stage that many people develop false images of God. The difficulties and problems at "A" become misinterpreted and misread to say that God is in some way unloving toward you. The God of perfect love becomes perceived as painfully unloving.

Negative God Images at "B" lead to emotional and behavioral *consequences* at "C." This is where the life struggles with depression, low self-esteem, fear, perfectionism, and anger come in. God seems to be unloving and because He is the most important figure in our lives we feel unlovable to some extent and then react by being depressed, unsure of ourselves, distrustful, perfectionistic, or angry.

Usually, we are aware of these discomforting consequences at "C" and want them removed. But you can't change your emotional and behavioral problems at "C" without changing the subconscious beliefs and perceptual sets at "B." This is the key to the whole thing, changing your perceptions and images of God! I gave you five steps to doing this in chapter 9. I also have designed what I call the "Eye Chart," which will help you focus your spiritual eyes on the God of love. Before we look at the Eye Chart we need to further investigate these types of distorted perceptual sets that cause problems at "B."

Negative Spiritual Self-Talk

Spiritual self-talk is what we tell ourselves about God.[1] When our self-talk about God becomes negative we develop distressful images of God. Usually our self-talk becomes negative in response to unwanted events or circumstances at stage "A." There are six types of negative self-talk at point "B" that lead to negative God Images. Each type is an irrational perceptual set that is intertwined with various emotional states. The six types of negative self-talk are:

1. Overgeneralization
2. Magnification
3. All-or-none reasoning
4. Selective abstraction
5. Personalization
6. Superstitious thinking

Overgeneralization This refers to the development of a general principle for all situations that is based on a misperception of a single event. Spiritually, this translates into blaming a difficult experience on God and generalizing your feelings and perceptions about that isolated experience to apply to the rest of your life. So one misperceived situation becomes the basis for all others. Overgeneralizations about God usually sound something like, "God never does such and such for me," "God always lets that happen to me," or, "Why won't God ever give me this certain thing I want?" Such statements have a tone of all-inclusiveness; they include words like *never* and *always*.

One man who was struggling to find a job said, "God didn't answer my prayer to give me that job I wanted so badly. He *never* answers my prayers. It's no use praying to Him because I *always* end up having to do things on my own anyway." He lost faith in God's supernaturally powerful and active love and was left with the Statue God. A young woman, who was plagued by the same type of negative self-talk, was stuck with a different false image of God. Her god was the Party-Pooper God. She complained, "My dream to be an actress didn't come true. God doesn't care about *any* of my dreams. He *always* disappoints me. It's obvious that He doesn't have *any* plans for my life. I have *no* hope for my future.''

These two people generalized misperceptions of God's involvement in a single issue to the rest of their lives. Generalizing misperceptions about God also commonly leads to distorted images of God as being a Preoccupied Managing Director God. You've probably heard people utter under their breath, ''God is *never* there for me when I need Him. He doesn't care about me.'' They generalize to all of life the instances in which they felt that God wasn't available for them.

Magnification This type of negative spiritual self-talk is based on fear rather than faith. Undesirable consequences that are feared are predicted to happen and then their effects are overestimated. This quickly leads to a self-fulfilling prophecy in which the feared thing happens. This is where the saying, ''The only thing you have to fear is fear itself'' comes from. A classic example of this is a sweet, little ''southern belle'' who is a devoutly spiritual woman but walks on spiritual eggshells because she is always afraid that the worst will happen. Her father developed cancer and she was stricken with fear that he'd die. She prayed and prayed but thought, *I'm afraid God won't heal my father's cancer. If He doesn't, then I'll know that He doesn't heal anymore.* She predicted that the worst would happen and then overestimated the effects to conclude that God isn't a healing God. Her God Image was really a variation of the Robber God who sneaks in and steals all you hold dear.

Another example of magnification can be heard in a teenage boy's cry, ''This church group better accept me. If they don't then I'm giving up on church and God. They probably won't. I guess I'm just not good enough for God or anyone else for that matter.'' He too feared the worst and exaggerated the effects of the predicted rejection until he had convinced himself he was worthless and God and Christians were ''too good'' for him. It's easy to see how this teenager's negative prediction would become a self-fulfilling prophecy in which the peers at church would reject him just as he had rejected himself. He clearly didn't feel loved by God. Instead, he magnified his misperception of God until he had a false image of an Elitist Aristocrat God who only associates with the "higher ups" in society.

All-or-none reasoning Many Christians have a need to put everything in life into extremes and absolutes. Things are white or black. There is no gray in life. They like to put life's complexities into nice, neat categories of all good or all bad. In their defense they may refer to Scriptures like Revelation 3:15, 16 in which John quotes Jesus as saying we must be hot or cold and that if we are lukewarm God will spit us out of His mouth. And certainly there is truth to this. Extremes of white and black, good and bad, hot and cold do exist and many things in life can be put into such categories. What these all-or-none people miss, though, are the numerous things in life that are "not so good" and "not so bad." In the parable of the wheat and tares (Matthew 13:24–30) Jesus referred to the sometimes close resemblance between good and evil. The wheat and tares look so similar that they must be harvested together. Extremists want to eliminate the tares before the harvest and end up eliminating some of the wheat by accident. Instead of letting God be the judge and tolerating a little uncertainty in life some people live by all-or-none reasoning.

Since so much of life doesn't fit into the tight little boxes of "all" or "none," people with this kind of dichotomized self-talk tend to develop distorted God Images. The most common expression of this is to think that you have to be a "total saint" to be accepted by God, that people are either angels or devils in God's sight. For people who think this way, actions are quickly categorized as "holy do's" or "sinful don'ts" without regard for the attitude and motive of the heart in the activity. Usually these people try to fit themselves into the "saint" category, but every now and then they slip into one of the "sinful don'ts." This can lead to incredible feelings of guilt or inadequacy. Suddenly God (in the voice of conscience) starts to sound like the Critical Scrooge, constantly condemning and putting them down. Or He may be clothed as the Vain Pharisee God who's nonaccepting of anything but total piety.

These same people may become perfectionists, anxiously striving to be "ideal saints." All the while, they fear making a mistake and becoming "devils" in the eyes of their God of Absolute Perfection who probably looks like the Outtagetcha Police Detective. Whatever the extremist's mistaken image of God, it stems from an anxious insecurity that requires life to fit into all-or-none categories in order for things to be okay.

Selective abstraction In this type of negative self-talk a conclusion is based on isolated details without considering contradictory evidence. A single event that is often misperceived is blown way out of proportion. God is blamed in the process, while indications of God's genuine love are ignored. This can happen when you focus on the things that God isn't doing for you and ignore the positive things that He is doing. When you do this it's not long before your troubles start to pile up and you begin to blame God for allowing bad things to happen to you: "Couldn't God have prevented this from happening to me?" "Why doesn't God protect me?" "I thought God answered prayer and wanted to bless me . . . why did He ignore my prayers and let that happen to me?" In the process the Lord becomes a Marshmallow God who is weak and helpless. God's power to "work all things together for good" and His awesome love revealed in big and small ways are overlooked.

Gregg is an example of someone who gave in to selective abstraction. Interestingly, he was Christian counselor, a good people-helper who was very active in ministering to the emotional well-being of his local church. Despite Gregg's benevolent heart, he was his own worst enemy. Like many Christian leaders, he tended to overemphasize his responsibilities as a servant of Christ to the point where he got out ahead of God, serving in his own strength rather than Christ's strength. He could not allow himself to be ministered to by others and to take time away from work to rest, be with his family, or just do something for himself.

Gregg was a "ministeraholic," a Christian workaholic ruled by an oppressive image of God as the Demanding Drill Sergeant God. He misunderstood Scripture to exhort him to "take God's yoke and burden upon himself" and to "carry other people's burdens" (*see* Matthew 11:29; Galatians 6:2). As a result Gregg was playing God and carrying the burden of the world on his own shoulders! He could never do enough. It was always, "do more and do it better." Gregg had overemphasized the importance of what he did for God and neglected the value of who he was for God and how he related to his Lord. The result was a faulty image of an impossible-to-please God.

Personalization This is when events are exaggerated and interpreted as relating to oneself when they don't. In this type of bad self-talk, you assume that things are directed at you when they're not. One woman who had a low self-esteem was convinced that God was condemning and criticizing her for not being a good enough Christian. She based this solely on her pastor's guilt-inducing sermons of threatened divine punishment. Out of fear and insecurity she mistakenly assumed that her pastor was preaching directly at her (he was so dogmatic that he was probably talking to himself). As a result she saw God as punitive and harsh like the Unjust Dictator God.

A different woman also had difficulty with her preacher. She was quick to feel taken advantage of and personalized the pushy and forceful altar calls of her minister. No matter what the purpose of the altar call, she went forward. She was afraid that if she didn't go forward God would be disappointed in her. She imagined God to be like the Pushy Salesman God.

Superstitious thinking The last type of negative self-talk that leads to destructive God Images is superstitious or magical thinking. Unrelated events are believed to have a magical cause-and-effect relationship. This type of spiritual self-talk turns God into a vending machine. Put a couple of quarters in and get your junk food out. God becomes a Magic Genie who grants your every self-centered wish so long as you rub Him the right way. This can take the subtle form of: "If I read my Bible and pray then God will bless me." The truth in that statement is distorted into the magical belief that you can get whatever you want by doing some certain thing. People who slip into this superstitious brand of Christianity may butter up God with good deeds or try to insure that their prayers will be answered by saying, "in Jesus' name," or, "I bind the devil."

Inevitably, superstitious Christians find that the "divine magic" doesn't always work. At such times they're likely to turn against their Magic Genie God. Their God Image may become a two-faced Indian Giver who cranks out the blessings and then all of a sudden pulls the rug out from under them. When the magic stops working they lose trust in God and blame Him for abandoning them or breaking His promises.

Improving Your Vision of God

Each form of spiritually destructive self-talk causes you to develop a negative God Image at point "B" of the A-B-C sequence. The reason for your unloving image of God isn't what has or hasn't happened to you at "A," but how you reacted to what has or hasn't happened to you at "B." It's your perceptual reaction to events and experiences that causes you to attribute unloving characteristics to God. The result of negative perceptions of God can be emotional distress and behavioral problems at "C." The obvious solution to destructive and distorted God Images is to seek a healing, renewal, and change in your image of God at "B." But how? How can you develop a more biblical perspective on what happens or doesn't happen to you? How can you gain better control of your emotions and actions? How can you see and feel the God of love when you're in distress?

To help answer these questions and combine the practical self-help steps suggested in chapter 9, we've developed the "Eye Chart" (*see* page 169). The Eye Chart is made to help you cope in times of distress or difficulty. It is divided into three rows and three columns, with the top row relating to your distorted God Images and the middle row to negative aspects in your self-image. The bottom row is for your "faith steps" to change unloving images of God and unlovable images of self. As for the columns, the first one on the left is for thoughts and feelings, the middle one for distorted perceptions, and one on the far right for new and positive perceptions.

To use your Eye Chart record your thoughts and feelings about God in the first column. Then, below that, list your thoughts and feelings about yourself. Next, in the middle column, reflect on and probe underneath your feelings to your perceptions. Identify and write down the name of your mistaken God Images and then the corresponding distorted self-concepts (*see* appendix I) that relate to your feelings and thoughts in the first column.

In the third column you identify the aspect of the Real God's love that your mistaken God Image distorts (*see* appendix II). Below that, identify the aspect of a healthy self-concept that can come from experiencing the aspect of God's perfect love that you identified above (*see* appendix I). This aspect of a lovable self should be opposite the distorted and unlovable self-concept in column two. Finally, in the third row at the bottom of the chart write down your "faith response." This might include a few of the action steps from chapter 9 that are focused on your particular "love need(s)."

The purpose of the Eye Chart is to help you gain a clearer picture of God and yourself. When you see God as He really is—in all His love and awesome glory—you can't help but feel and believe that you are lovable to Him. Jesus said that your eyes are the lamp of your body. If your eyes are full of light all of you will be full of light. If your eyes are bad and cannot see the light then all of you will be full of darkness (Matthew 6:22, 23). Jesus Himself is the Light. We need to see this Divine Light of love and glory so that we can receive the goodness of God into our hearts and be full of the Light. Most of us have trouble really seeing the light of God's love with our naked eyes. We need glasses—the

EYE CHART

I THINK & FEEL ABOUT GOD	MISTAKEN GOD IMAGES (appendix I)	REAL GOD (appendix II)
I THINK & FEEL ABOUT MYSELF	NEGATIVE SELF-IMAGES (appendix I)	LOVABLE SELF (appendix II)

FAITH RESPONSE (action steps from chapter 9)

SAMPLE EYE CHART

I THINK & FEEL ABOUT GOD:	MISTAKEN GOD IMAGES (*see* appendix I)	REAL GOD (*see* appendix II):
God is too busy for me. He doesn't really care about what is going on in my life.	Preoccupied Managing Director God	Patient God: always available to me and concerned about me.
God won't intervene to help me in this situation. I'll have to work things out for myself.	Statue God	Actively Kind God: will freely and kindly act on my behalf.
God only loves me if I do what He wants. If I play His game and meet His conditions He has to bless me.	Magic Genie God	Unconditional God: loves me just as I am.
God is so harsh and demanding with me. When I think I've pleased Him He asks for more.	Demanding Drill Sergeant God	Considerate God: is considerate of my needs and doesn't demand more than I can do.
I THINK & FEEL ABOUT MYSELF:	**NEGATIVE SELF-IMAGES (*see* appendix I)**	**LOVABLE SELF (*see* appendix II):**
I'm not worth God's availability and concern for the details of my life.	I'm forgotten and neglected.	I'm Wanted: I'm worth God's time and patient concern.
I'm not worth God's active help and intervention in my life. My needs aren't important to Him. I have to take care of myself.	I don't get helped.	I'm Helped: I don't have to do everything on my own because God cares about my needs and is able and wanting to help me.
I'm not worth being loved just for me. It's up to me to make God love me.	I have to be in control.	I'm Loved Unconditionally: I'm worth being loved by God as I am.
I'm not acceptable to God unless I measure up to His demands. I can't do enough to please Him.	I must do more.	I'm Acceptable: I'm worth being accepted by God for who I am. I don't have to earn His acceptance.

I WILL RESPOND IN FAITH BY DOING THE FOLLOWING THINGS (*see* chapter 9):

1. Receive God's love for me through my wife who wants me, is helpful toward me, loves me unconditionally, and accepts me.
2. Meditate on promises and examples from the Bible that reveal the Patient God, Actively Kind God, Unconditional God, and Considerate God to me. As I grow in my knowledge of the truth of God's love for me I'll be set free from Satan's lies about God that come in the form of Mistaken God Images.
3. Express my feelings to God in my prayer. I accept the fact that I struggle to feel God's perfect love sometimes and will express these painful feelings and questions to God in prayer.
4. I will continually ask God in prayer to help me receive His patient, actively kind, unconditional, and considerate love.
5. Visually and prayerfully meditate on Psalm 23 and John 10:1–18 in which God is revealed as a loving shepherd toward me, His priceless sheep, and also on Luke 15:11–31 in which God is shown to be a loving Father toward me, His special child. In each of these pictures of God's love for me I specifically see His patient, actively kind, unconditional, and considerate love.

glasses of meditation on Scripture, prayer, and relationships with godly and loving people.

A Prayer

I pray that God may give you His Spirit of wisdom and revelation so that you would really see and know the glorious riches of His love for you. If you'd receive this precious Spirit, the eyes of your heart would be so enlightened by the bright and ever-shining Light of His love. I know that sometimes dark clouds dim the Light from above in your life. You forget though that as God's child you already have His Light within to help you in those dark days. You have also the lamp of His Word to Light your darkened path. Most of all, you have the assurance that the Son is always shining. Only sometimes you don't see Him shine from where you stand.

Don't give up, my friend! Though the dark clouds may block the Son's light and the cold wind may blow out your lamp's light, nothing can block or blow out the Light of Christ within! This Light is your eternal gift as a son or daughter of the Light. I pray that you won't hide this Light under a bushel. Oh, that you would lift the bushel and uncover the very depths of your heart; even your pains and your fears. Then you will see that you are not alone in your pain and fear.

I know this isn't easy. This is why I pray for you. I pray that you would find strength through the inner Light God has given you. This inner Light is the power of God's Companion Spirit in your inner being. It's only by faith that you can let the Light of the Son shine in your heart on a dark, cold, and windy day. If you'd reach inside and make yourself known to God and others you will receive the Companion Light you need and will grow to be rooted and established in God's love. You'll have power, together with all the saints, to know this love that surpasses knowledge. Through faith in Christ's power that is at work within, you will be filled to the measure of all the fullness of God.

Questions for Reflection and Discussion

1. Read the story of when "Doubting Thomas" heard of Jesus' resurrection in John 20:24–29. What might Thomas's spiritual self-talk have sounded like during the week between the time he was told of the resurrection and the time Jesus appeared to Thomas? What do you suppose his image of God was during that week?

2. Read Psalm 42. Do you think there is a connection between how the writer feels distanced from God (vv. 2, 3, 9) and also feels depressed and discouraged (vv. 5, 9–11)? The writer cries out for God (vv. 1, 2), searches his feelings (vv. 3, 5, 10, 11), remembers better times in the past (v. 4), considers the persecutions of his enemies (vv. 3, 10), confronts God (v. 9), and tries to put his hope in God (v. 11). Many people would say this Psalm has a "negative" tone. Would you say this is an example of good or bad self-talk? Why?

3. Read Proverbs 10:24 and 2 Timothy 1:7. Spiritual self-talk can be either "fear-talk" or "faith-talk." Rate from 1 to 10 the way you talk to yourself when you're stressed or undergoing a difficult time. Let 1 be extremely fearful, worried, pessimistic, and doubtful self-talk and let 10 be extremely faith-focused, confident, optimistic, and hopeful self-talk.

4. Which of the six types of negative self-talk in chapter 10 do you struggle with most in your spiritual life? How does this impact your image of God?

5. Using a specific example from a time you struggled with a distorted God Image try to identify the A-B-C's of what went wrong, and then change your self-talk at "B" and consider how the consequences at "C" might have been different.

6. Using the same example you used in question 5 (or a different example if you prefer), try filling out the Eye Chart. Can you see a connection between how you think and feel about God and how you think and feel about yourself?

11
Letting God Be God

Be still, and know that I am God.

Psalms 46:10

No matter what our image of God is, God is still God. We can't create God and we can't change God. We only create an image, a picture in our hearts, of what He is like. We strive to see Him as He is—a perfectly loving God. We all fail miserably though, seeing only a "poor reflection" of God in this life (1 Corinthians 13:12). At best we are left clinging to a picture that is something like God. For, when Jesus ascended into heaven the only perfect image of God left us. The Father then sent the Holy Spirit, the Spirit of Jesus, to replace the God-man. Now the closest thing to God in the flesh that we have to encourage our faith in the invisible God is one another indwelt by the Holy Spirit. So when you love me you reveal God to me, you make His Word take on flesh and bones. Then I am helped to create a more accurate God Image. The picture of God that I had outlined from my knowledge of the Bible starts to be filled in. God's love becomes more than just "words on a page." I not only know about God's love, but I also know of His love from experience. We need both.

Often, though, we don't have both. We know about His love but don't feel or experience it. Usually this is because of destructive, painful, or inadequate relationships with people whom we needed to represent God's love to us. This is when we struggle, when we may start to doubt that He really loves us. At such times we are prone to draw in our hearts a bad picture of His love and create a negative and inaccurate God Image. This is the testing of our faith. We need this too.

When your faith is tested and you feel that you don't have what you need from God you must remember that His ways are higher than our ways. Our human minds do not always understand the divine mind. Sometimes we must be satisfied with uncertainty and unanswered questions. You have the right to doubt God's love, to question your Lord; we all do it. Some of us just try to hide it from ourselves and everyone else. But God knows, so tell Him how you feel. Tell Him about all the injustices, the pain, the confusion, the temptation. He will listen.

He listened to one poor suffering soul who decided to give God just what he had dished out to mankind. He saw another side to the great decalogue. So he wrote out ten new commandments that he demanded God follow:

> Thou shalt love man as much as man loves thee.
> Thou shalt honor thy promise to Noah.
> Thou shalt protect all children from every natural harm.
> Thou shalt ease childbirth's travail.
> Thou shalt match man's pace toward peace.
> Thou shalt not cause the birth of crippled children.
> Thou shalt not steal children from their parents.
> Thou shalt not cause the poor, the innocent, or the faithful to suffer famine.
> Thou shalt not harden any man's heart.

Thou shalt not test one man more than any other man.
Amen.[1]

An American Prisoner

If God would abide by these seemingly just commandments then everything would be fine, wouldn't it? No problems. No pain. Everything would be fair and equal. What we would have though would be a world of robots existing in a plastic bubble. There would be no need for faith in God. No need for relationship with your Creator. No need even for God! In such a world of sterile and exact "fairness" you would be your own god. Better to have a world of pain, problems, confusion, unfairness, and still be able to fight for faith and life itself.

Life does get bad though sometimes, doesn't it? (If yours doesn't then maybe you've created a bubble for yourself to shelter you from life's difficulties.) I had a bad day not too long ago. I even muttered a complaint or two upwards in God's direction. A friend shared with me a poem he wrote which gave me perspective on my bad day that I thought was so "God-awful."

A God-awful day. . . .

One wag said it was a God-awful day,
I agreed,
until I read how it is to be
when God gets awful----
then I perceived how our perception of awful
(attributed to God or not)
is merely rudimentary.

Even the Devil, if I see it rightly,
is greatly less able
to be God-awful in his awfulness,
seeing he is less,
and only, as it were
an instrument (self appointed, if you prefer)
of awfulness,

but, rather, 'tis He, the Creator
who in wrath can rage more fully,
more awfully.

So, even tho' the Devil is a roaring lion
devouring God's creatures,
'Tis God who will cast lion, gut-filled and all
into hell.
Now that's God-awful!

So, altho' today was bad,
and tomorrow promises
to be bleak,
such awfulness is just the rudiments.

Let us not judge so soon ----
that's what the Devil did ----
and misjudged.
Now, he knows what God-awful means ---
Let us determine not to know
as he.[2]

When you feel that God is awful be careful. Don't ignore your feelings. Also, don't make the opposite mistake and conclude that your feelings are more than your own inner reality; they describe how you feel, not necessarily how God is. If you make either of these two mistakes you are likely to misjudge God just as the devil did. The devil experienced God's wrathful judgment because he judged God as bad and himself as better. His distorted image of God became a self-fulfilling prophecy that destroyed him. He experienced real God-awfulness! We need to be careful about our distorted images of God. If they're either hidden or accepted as truth, they gain power over us and keep us from experiencing God's love. To avoid such God-awfulness, honestly acknowledge your feelings and work them through. Most of all, remember that there is a God who is a good God, a God of perfect love. When you're having a bad day be careful not to judge God too soon, lest you discover real God-awfulness!

You've probably heard the saying, "I never promised you a rose garden." Well, God never promised us life without pain and struggle. Job was a righteous man. He was considered to have the greatest faith in God and be the most righteous of any person in his day. Compared to other people he didn't deserve the terrible suffering that God allowed Satan to inflict on him. It's easy for us to understand how Job blamed God for his misery and developed a distorted God Image. If we can learn anything from Job, it's that we will encounter pain and difficulty in this life. The issue is not whether or not we can avoid such problems, but whether we can maintain faith in a loving God in their midst. It is possible—though not at all easy—for you to reach up to God in faith and know His love even in the midst of your own personal "hell on earth." A. W. Tozer calls this upward reach "the gaze of the soul," the moment when you realize, "Thou God seest me." Surely, "When the eyes of the soul looking out meet the eyes of God looking in, heaven has begun right here on this earth."[3]

Developing and maintaining a more loving image of God won't protect you from the necessity of confronting your own personal hells on earth. It will make your problems easier to bear though. Just ask Job! He learned his lesson the hard way. After much suffering he finally found the sweet communion with his Loving Lord that turns the darkest hell into the brightest heaven. Had he found God's love sooner, he still would have suffered, but his outward suffering would have been met with inward peace. This is life's greatest challenge: to maintain a genuine heartfelt faith in God's love in the midst of great difficulty.

So the key for you is to get a glimpse of God as really being with you in your life struggles. Depending upon what you're going through, you may need to see God in any of a number of the ways He reveals Himself: a gentle and tender Father, an understanding and supportive Mother, a Good Shepherd to guide you, a trusted Friend, a Master who accepts you into His family, a Potter to mold you into something special, a Vinedresser to help you be more fruitful, a Gold Refiner to purify you, a Bridegroom to marry you, a Brother to walk alongside you, a Deliverer, a Healer, or a bright ray of Sunlight. Whatever image of God you best relate to, it is a good image if it leads you to the One True God who is far bigger than and different from any picture you may have of what He is like. A good God Image is simply an aid to help you understand what the infinite, eternal, and Almighty God is really like. It's the God behind our picture that we worship. To do otherwise and worship our picture of God rather than God Himself would be idolatry.

One writer described our images of God as being like Jacob's ladder.[4] They can lead us up or down—closer to God or farther away from Him. But in the end they are only pictures of what He is really like and are limited because they can never lead us all the way to God. Where the ladder ends there is a gap. God steps into that gap in the person of Jesus Christ in order to reach us. We too must step into the gap—taking a step of faith toward God's reaching hands. Sometimes it's a step into the dark. Always it feels like a risk. You must trust that when you step into the gap Jesus will catch you!

Appendix I

Unloving God Images and Unlovable Self-Images

Unloving God Image	Unlovable Self-Image
PREOCCUPIED MANAGING DIRECTOR GOD: is responsible to run the world and your life, but doesn't take the time or energy to be involved with you; is impatient and unavailable.	I'M FORGOTTEN AND NEGLECTED: I'm not worth God's time and concern, the details of my life don't fit into His busy schedule; I can't disturb God with my problems.
STATUE GOD: doesn't move to help you, but leaves you to work out things on your own; distant, impersonal, uncaring, refuses to act kindly on your behalf.	I DON'T GET HELPED: I'm not worth God's active help and intervention in my life so I have to manage on my own; I can't get close to God, my wants and needs aren't important to Him.
ROBBER GOD: takes good things away from you, jealous of your good fortune, a "killjoy" and a "spoilsport" who ruins your good times.	I MUST GET ALL I CAN AND HANG ON: I'm not worth God's support and encouragement; I don't deserve good things; if I don't hang on to what I have, God will take it away from me.

Unloving God Image	Unlovable Self-Image
VAIN PHARISEE GOD: brags on himself and puts you down; expects you to humiliate yourself and give him constant homage; takes credit for your successes.	I ALWAYS GET PUT DOWN: I'm not worth God's esteem and praise; I should put myself down so God can be glorified; I don't deserve any credit for anything so God takes it all.
ELITIST ARISTOCRAT GOD: considers himself unneeding of you and too good to associate with you; an elitist snob.	I GET EXCLUDED AND LEFT OUT: I'm not good enough to be included in God's elite crowd. I'm not acceptable to Him; He doesn't need me for anything.
PUSHY SALESMAN GOD: rudely and shamefully pushes you to do things his way, violating and using you; forces himself on you, smothers you.	I GET PUSHED AROUND: I'm worthless and cheap in God's eyes; I deserve to be taken advantage of; I should be ashamed to be me; I can't say no to God; if I don't watch out God will force me to do something I don't want to do.
MAGIC GENIE GOD: gives you good things if you do things his way; does whatever you want him to if you follow the right formula.	I HAVE TO BE IN CONTROL: I'm not worth being loved by God just for me, but have to do certain things to get God to love and help me; I can get God to do whatever I want if I play His game.

Unloving God Image	Unlovable Self-Image
DEMANDING DRILL SERGEANT GOD: always demands more and more from you, is never quite satisfied with you; gets angry and harsh with you if you don't meet his expectations; won't tolerate mistakes, weaknesses, or failures.	I MUST DO MORE: I'm not worth being accepted by God unless I meet His demands. I can never do enough to earn His love and respect; I must be the best, always win, do everything right; if I mess up, I make up.
OUTTAGETCHA POLICE DETECTIVE GOD: perfectionistic and legalistic; looks to catch you slip up; holds your sin against you and won't forgive you.	I HAVE TO BE PERFECT: I'm not worth being accepted as imperfect; I have to be careful or I'll get caught making a mistake; I'm not given a second chance or forgiven.
UNJUST DICTATOR GOD: an unfair authority who lords his power over you; punishes you even if you're good and blesses others even if they're bad; doesn't punish those who hurt you.	I'M NOT TREATED FAIRLY: I'm not worth fair treatment from God; I always get a raw deal; I deserve to be punished by God even when I'm good; I don't deserve for God to stand up for me when I've been wronged and treated unjustly.
MARSHMALLOW GOD: weak and ineffectual, doesn't protect you or stand up for you; may overprotect you and treat you like a baby.	I'M VULNERABLE TO HARM: I'm not worthy being protected by God; I'm dependent and helpless so I must stay away from danger.

Unloving God Image

CRITICAL SCROOGE GOD: disbelieves in and disrespects you; won't commit to help you, but stands back and criticizes you; tells you, "You won't make it," and "You can't do it."

PARTY-POOPER GOD: is negative, pessimistic, and hopeless about you and your life; tells you, "It won't work," and "Nothing will work for you."

INDIAN GIVER GOD: is an inconsistent heartbreaker; backs away from you when you need him; breaks his promises to you.

Unlovable Self-Image

I'M NOT CONFIDENT: I'm not worth God's respect and trust; I deserve to be criticized and put down for all my failures; I'll never amount to anything; I can't do anything well.

I DON'T HAVE HOPE: I'm not worth God's having a special plan and purpose for my life; my dreams and hopes aren't important to God; nothing works out the way I want it to.

I GET LET DOWN: I'm not worth God's consistent and steadfast care; I'm afraid to trust God lest He leave me when I need Him most; I never get what God promises me.

Appendix II

Loving God Images and Lovable Self-Images

Loving God Image	Lovable Self-Image
PATIENT GOD: God is patient and personable with me and always available for me; He is concerned about even the little details of my life.	I'M WANTED: I'm worth God's time and concern; I'm so important to God that He is personally involved in the details of my life.
ACTIVELY KIND GOD: God acts kindly and graciously on my behalf, giving freely of Himself; He takes initiative to personally relate to me.	I'M HELPED: I'm worth God's active help and intervention in my life; I don't have to manage on my own because when I need help God is there for me; God loves me enough to relate personally with me.
GIVING GOD: God gives me good things; He contributes to my well-being; He never jealously withholds or takes things from me; He doesn't ruin my fun.	I'M CARED FOR: I'm worth God's support and encouragement; I can trust that God will give me only what is good for me and will bless me; I don't need to cling to what I have, but can give freely.

Loving God Image	Lovable Self-Image
PRAISING GOD: God praises and exalts me as His child; He doesn't boast on Himself, but seeks to build me up.	I'M PRAISED: I'm worth being esteemed and praised by God; it's good for me to receive praise for who I am and what I've done "in Christ" and to God's glory.
HUMBLE GOD: God humbly seeks to associate Himself with me and to include me in what He does; He allows Himself to "need" me.	I'M INCLUDED: I'm worth being included in God's company, I've been chosen to be a part of His privileged family; I'm needed and important to God.
GENTLE GOD: God gently seeks to be intimate with me without pushing Himself on me; God respects me as an individual; He isn't rude or shameful.	I'M VALUED: I'm priceless and valuable in God's eyes, I deserve to be treated with gentleness and respect; God gives me the right to say no; I'll protect the value of my identity as God's child.
UNCONDITIONAL GOD: God loves me just as I am; He doesn't love me conditionally upon my doing certain things; He does what is best for me, not what some formula says He should do.	I'M LOVED AS I AM: I'm worth being loved just as I am; there is nothing I have to do to get God to love me; I can't control or obligate God, but receive what I need from Him by simple faith.

Loving God Image

Lovable Self-Image

ACCEPTING GOD: God accepts me regardless of my performance; He is considerate and understanding of my struggles; He isn't harsh or overly demanding, but is flexible.

I'M ACCEPTABLE: I'm worth being accepted by God even if I'm not a success; I don't have to earn God's love or make up for my mistakes; God helps me to achieve success.

MERCIFUL GOD: God mercifully forgives me for my failures and doesn't hold them against me; He doesn't look to catch me doing wrong; He doesn't want to punish me; He is perfect but not a perfectionist.

I'M FORGIVEN: I'm worth being forgiven and trusted to do right by God; I'm worth a second chance; I'm helped by God to avoid sin; I'm accepted based on Christ's perfection not my imperfection.

FAIR GOD: God is holy, just, and honest; He is a fair authority who disciplines me for my good; He blesses me for serving Him; He punishes those who unjustly wrong me.

I'M FAIRLY GOVERNED: I'm worth being treated fairly by God; I'm disciplined by God only in love and for my good; I'm rewarded by God for my faithfulness to Him; I deserve for God to stand up for me when I've been wronged.

PROTECTOR GOD: God protects me from harm and gives me freedom and responsibility when I'm ready for it; He preserves the life He's given me.

I'M PROTECTED: I'm worth being protected by God; I am a responsible adult in God's eyes; God guides and protects my life as I step out in new challenges.

Loving God Image

RESPECTING GOD: God fully believes in and respects my ability to do what I need and want to do; God commits Himself to my welfare, helping me succeed.

HOPEFUL GOD: God is hopeful and optimistic that my future will be bright, my plans will work, and my dreams will come true; He has a plan for my life that brings glory to Him.

STEADFAST GOD: God is eternally and consistently reliable. He perseveres with and supports me even if it causes Him to suffer; He gives Himself to me without fail, never breaking His promises.

Lovable Self-Image

I'M BELIEVED IN: I'm worth God's respect; I'm worth God's committing Himself to help me succeed; I can accomplish many good things with God's help; it is good for my successes to be recognized by God.

I'M HOPED FOR: I'm worth being given a special purpose and hope by God; my dreams are important to God; things will work out for me in the way that is best.

I'M SECURE: I'm worth God's consistent and secure support; I don't need to fear because God is always with me, even in trouble; I always receive God's promises in their time.

Source Notes

Chapter 1: What Is Your Image of God?

1. Idries Shah, *Caravan of Dreams* (Baltimore: Penguin, 1972), p. 172.
2. David Seamands, *Healing of Memories* (Wheaton, Ill.: Victor Books, 1985), p. 95.
3. Ann Belford Ulanov, *Picturing God* (Cambridge: Cowley Publications, 1986), p. 164.
4. This term is most widely used in the psychodynamic school of psychology. *See* especially Anna-Maria Rizzuto's book *Birth of the Living God* (Chicago: University of Chicago Press, 1979). Also, John McDargh's book *Psychoanalytic Object Relations Theory and the Study of Religion: On Faith and the Imaging of God* (New York: University Press of America, 1983). These and many other works related to God Images were summarized in my Ph.D. dissertion for United States International University, "The Preliminary Development and Validation of a Measure of God Images." (University Microfilms International, 1989).
5. Os Guiness, *In Two Minds* (Downers Grove, Ill.: Inter-Varsity Press, 1976), p. 87.
6. For the complete version of the God Image Questionnaire see my Ph.D. dissertation (University Microfilms International, 1989).
7. A. W. Tozer, *The Knowledge of the Holy* (New York: Harper & Row, 1961), p. 10.
8. Aaron L. Rutledge, "Concepts of God Among the Emotionally Upset," *Pastoral Psychology, 2*, 1951, p. 22.
9. J. B. Phillips, *Your God Is Too Small* (New York: Macmillan Publishing Company, 1961) . p. 7.
10. Tozer, *Knowledge of the Holy*, p. 6.

Chapter 2: Meeting Fourteen False Gods

1. J. B. Phillips *Your God Is Too Small* (New York, Macmillan Publishing Company, 1961), p. 40.
2. Ibid., pp. 42–43.
3. David Seamands, *Healing of Memories* (Wheaton, Ill.: Victor Books. 1985), p. 105.
4. Joseph Sica, "Will the Real God Please Stand Up?" *Marriage and Family Living,* August 1983, p. 20.
5. Phillips, *Your God Is Too Small,* p. 56.
6. Ibid., p. 57.
7. John G. Stackhouse, Jr., "Your God Is Too Middle-Sized," *Christianity Today,* June 13, 1986, p. 23.
8. Seamands, *Healing of Memories*, p. 105.
9. Sica, "Will the Real God Please Stand Up?" p. 18.
10. Phillips, *Your God Is Too Small,* p. 15.
11. Ibid., p. 33.
12. Ibid., p. 48.

Chapter 3: Creating God in Your Parents' Image

1. Anna-Maria Rizzuto, *The Birth of the Living God* (Chicago: University of Chicago Press, 1979), p. 8.
2. J. B. Phillips, *Your God Is Too Small* (New York: Macmillan Publishing Company, 1961), p. 19.
3. Diane Long, David Elkind, and Bernard Spilka, "The Child's Conception of Prayer," *Journal for the Scientific Study of Religion, 6,* 1967, pp. 101–109.
4. V. Madge, *Children in Search of Meaning* (New York: Morehouse-Barlow, 1966), p. 14.
5. Daniel J. Heinrichs, "Our Father Which Art in Heaven: Parataxic Distortions in the Image of God," *Journal of Psychology and Theology, 10*(2), 1982, p. 128.
6. John McDargh, *Psychoanalytic Object Relations Theory and the Study of Religion* (New York: University Press of America, 1983), p. 132.
7. Carl Barshinger, "Intimacy and Spiritual Growth," *The Christian Association for Psychological Studies Bulletin,* 2, 1977, p. 20.
8. Leigh C. Bishop, "The Dream of the Magician: A Case of Parataxic Distortion," *Journal of Psychology and Christianity, 4*(2), 1985, pp. 12–14.

9. Phillips, *Your God Is Too Small,* p. 15.
10. Bruce Narramore, *No Condemnation* (Grand Rapids: Zondervan, 1984).
11. Os Guiness, *In Two Minds* (Downers Grove, Ill.: Inter-Varsity Press, 1976).
12. David Seamands, *Healing of Memories* (Wheaton, Ill.: Victor Books, 1985), p. 97.
13. Philip Yancey, *Where Is God When It Hurts?* (Grand Rapids: Zondervan, 1977).
14. Harold Kushner, *When Bad Things Happen to Good People* (New York: Schocken Books, Inc., 1981).
15. Lewis Smedes, *Forgive and Forget* (New York: Harper & Row, 1984).

Chapter 4: When Will God Wipe Away My Tears?

1. Os Guiness, *In Two Minds* (Downers Grove, Ill.: Inter-Varsity Press, 1976), p. 95.
2. Philip Yancey, *Where Is God When It Hurts?* (Grand Rapids: Zondervan, 1977), p. 63.
3. C. S. Lewis, *A Grief Observed* (New York: Bantam Books, 1961), pp. 4, 5.
4. J. B. Phillips, *Your God Is Too Small* (New York: Macmillan Publishing Company, 1961), p. 48.
5. W. Bingham Hunter, "Why Pray to a God Who Lets People Hurt?" *Connections,* Biola University, Spring 1988, p. 3.
6. Paul Brand and Philip Yancey, *In His Image* (Grand Rapids: Zondervan, 1984), pp. 279, 280.
7. Pierre Wolff, *May I Hate God?* (New York: Paulist Press, 1979), p. 35.

Chapter 5: Worming Our Way to God

1. David Burns, *Feeling Good: The New Mood Therapy* (New York: New American Library, 1979), p. 14
2. S. Bruce Narramore, *You're Someone Special* (Grand Rapids: Zondervan, 1974), p. 21.
3. David Stoop, *Living With a Perfectionist* (Nashville: Thomas Nelson, 1987), p. 70.
4. Myron R. Chartier and Larry A. Goehner, "A Study of the

Relationship of Parent-Adolescent Communication, Self-Esteem, and God Image,'' *Journal of Psychology and Theology, 4*(3), 1976, pp. 227–232. Jerry C. Jolley and Steven J. Taulbee, ''Assessing Perceptions of Self and God: Comparison of Prisoners and Normals,'' *Psychological Reports, 59,* 1986, pp. 1139–1146.
5. Peter Benson and Bernard Spilka, ''God Image as a Function of Self-Esteem and Locus of Control,'' *Journal for the Scientific Study of Religion, 12,* 1973, pp. 297–310.
6. Stoop, *Living With a Perfectionist,* p. 155.

Chapter 6: Can I Really Trust God?

1. David Seamands, *Healing of Memories* (Wheaton, Ill.: Victor Books, 1985), p. 111.
2. William G. Justice and Warren Lambert, ''A Comparative Study of the Language People Use to Describe the Personalities of God and Their Earthly Parents,'' *The Journal of Pastoral Care,* June 1986, *40* (2), pp. 166–172.
3. Ibid., p. 166.
4. Ibid.
5. Sharon Abercrombie, ''12-Step Minister Hopes to Make a Difference,'' *Changes: For Adult Children of Alcoholics,* July–August 1988, p. 11.
6. Os Guiness, *In Two Minds* (Downers Grove, Ill.: Inter-Varsity Press, 1976), pp. 84, 85.

Chapter 7: I Have to Be Perfect . . .

1. David A Stoop, *Living With a Perfectionist* (Nashville: Thomas Nelson, 1987), p. 16.
2. J. B. Phillips, *Your God Is Too Small* (New York: Macmillan Publishing Company, 1961), p. 32.
3. David Seamands, *Healing for Damaged Emotions* (Wheaton, Ill.: Victor Books, 1981), p. 78.
4. Stoop, *Living With a Perfectionist,* p. 154.
5. Phillips, *Your God Is Too Small,* p. 30.
6. Seamands, *Healing for Damaged Emotions,* p. 80.
7. Stoop, *Living With a Perfectionist,* p. 158.
8. Leigh C. Bishop, ''The Dream of the Magician: A Case of

Parataxic Distortion,'' *Journal of Psychology and Christianity, 4* (2), 1985, p. 12.

9. Seamands, *Healing for Damaged Emotions*, pp. 82, 83.
10. Ibid., p. 81.
11. Karen Horney, *Neurosis and Human Growth* (New York: W. W. Norton, 1950), p. 176.
12. Seamands, *Healing for Damaged Emotions*, p. 103.
13. Stoop, *Living With a Perfectionist,* p. 157.
14. Frances J. White, ''Earthly Father/Heavenly Father,'' *Journal of Psychology and Christianity, 4* (2), 1985, p. 79.

Chapter 8: Shhh! I'm Angry at God!

1. Pierre Wolff, *May I Hate God?* (New York: Paulist Press, 1979), p. 28.
2. Lewis Smedes, *Forgive and Forget* (New York: Harper & Row, 1984), p. 111.
3. Wolff, *May I Hate God?* pp. 31, 32.
4. David Seamands, *Healing for Damaged Emotions* (Wheaton, Ill.: Victor Books, 1981), p. 96, 97.
5. Don Postema, *Space for God* (Grand Rapids: Bible Way, 1983), p. 134.
6. William Edkins, ''Psychoanalysis and Religious Experience,'' *Journal of Psychology and Christianity, 4* (2), 1985, pp. 86, 87.
7. *See* for example, Psalms 10:15; 18:6–15; 31:17; 35:1–28; 54:5; 56:5–7; 58:6–8; 69:19–28; 70:13.

Chapter 9: Seeing a New Image of God

1. Agnes Sanford, *The Healing Gifts of the Spirit* (New York: Harper & Row, 1966).
2. A. W. Tozer, *The Knowledge of the Holy* (New York: Harper & Row, 1961), p. 16.
3. David Stoop, *Self-Talk: Key to Personal Growth* (Old Tappan, N.J.: Fleming H. Revell Company, 1982).
4. For further discussion of Christian meditation, consult chapter 2 of Richard Foster's book *Celebration of Discipline* (New York: Harper & Row, 1978).

Chapter 10: The A-B-C's of a Loving God Image

1. David Stoop's book *Self-Talk: Key to Personal Growth* (Old Tappan, N.J.: Fleming H. Revell Company, 1982) will help you improve your self-talk.

Chapter 11: Letting God Be God

1. Quoted in Pierre Wolff's *May I Hate God?* (New York: Paulist Press, 1979), p. 4.
2. H. Keith Ewing, Assistant Professor of English, Southern California College, Costa Mesa, California. Used by permission of the author.
3. A. W. Tozer, *The Pursuit of God* (Camp Hill, Penn.: Christian Publications, Inc., 1982), p. 92.
4. Ann Belford Ulanov, *Picturing God* (Cambridge: Cowley Publications, 1986), p. 176.